Millions Now Living Will Never Die!

Predictions of the Jehovah's Witnesses and the Watch Tower Society

By J. F. Rutherford

Published by Pantianos Classics

ISBN-13: 978-1-78987-286-6

First published between 1918 and 1920

Contents

Prefatory

Judge J. F. Rutherford,
Brooklyn, N. Y.

Dear Sir:

The advance proof pages of your brochure, "Millions Now Living Will Never Die", which you kindly allowed me to read, have proved to be even more interesting than hoped for, and I embrace this early opportunity to express to you my sincere appreciation of the work. The admirable way in which you have marshalled the sayings of the Lord Jesus, of the apostles, and of the prophets of old, and supported them by abundant secular evidence, all going to show that a time would come when millions then living would never die - and that we are now living in that time - will inspire hope and confidence in the mind of every honest, truth seeking reader.

As the one who had the esteemed privilege of syndicating Pastor Russell's sermons in thousands of newspapers in many lands, I was naturally anxious to know how you would treat the prophecies so often referred to in Pastor Russell's sermons. I am glad, indeed, to note that you treat the major part of your evidence from the standpoint of fulfilled prophecy. For one, I am glad that you gathered such an array of evidence to substantiate your claims and to show the people, as a basis for the worth-while hope, how they may live for ever. It will not be necessary for anyone to consider your statement as a guess.

Again thanking you and wishing you rich eternal blessings for your labor of love, I subscribe myself as

Yours in the best of bonds,

G. C. DRISCOLL
Santa Monica Calif.,
May 17, 1920

Millions Now Living Will Never Die

THE emphatic announcement that millions now living on earth will never die must seem presumptuous to many people; but when the evidence is carefully considered I believe that almost every fair mind will concede that the conclusion is a reasonable one.

For nearly nineteen hundred years Christians have been looking forward to a time coming when life everlasting will be offered to all the peoples of earth. Their expectations and hopes have been based upon the combined testimony of the inspired prophets of old -from Moses to John-upon the testimony of Jesus of Nazareth, the Son of the living God, and upon the testimony of his inspired apostles.

About 4,000 years ago God made a promise to Abraham in which he said that he would bless Abraham and through his seed all the families of the earth should be blessed. Not only did he make this promise, but he bound it with his oath; and St. Paul plainly tells us that these two things, God's word and oath are unchangeable, and that his promises must be fulfilled. Based upon that oathbound promise and subsequent like promises made to the offspring of Abraham, devout Jews of the world have since looked forward to the time coming when blessings of life and happiness eternal will be offered to mankind.

Today the eyes of orthodox Jews of earth are fixed upon Palestine. They are looking up and lifting up their heads and the hope is springing into millions of hearts that the time is at hand for the regathering of the Jews to Palestine and the establishment there of a state or government of the Jews and for the Jews, according to the divine arrangement. Since the time of Abraham they have looked for the Messiah, but have not yet discerned who constitutes the Messiah.

Life everlasting in a state of happiness is the greatest desire of all men. Whether men have faith or not in the divine promises, each one would be glad to know for a certainty that there was before him life everlasting in a happy state. In view of this strong desire, and of the cumulative evidence given by the holy men of old concerning such coming blessings, it seems strange that more people have not tried to inform themselves upon the subject. The reason, as assigned by the Apostle Paul, is that "the god of this world [Satan, the invisible ruler of the present social order of things] hath blinded the minds of those who are perishing, lest the glorious glad tidings of Christ Jesus, who is the image of God, should shine into their hearts".- 2 Corinthians 4:4. Many men of ability in the past centuries have entered the Christian ministry. The great adversary, knowing their vulnerable points, has used others to flatter and cajole them and to turn their minds toward worldly things, and by far the greater number of these clergymen, yielding to the baneful and seductive influence of the adversary, have themselves turned away from the Bible, and have blindly led the people in the wrong direction. They seem to have lost sight entirely of the fact that God has a great plan which he is causing to work out in an orderly, majestic manner. But the hour has struck when the people shall know the truth, and they that know the truth shall be made free from the bondage of ignorance and superstition and their minds shall be turned into the channels leading to unending joy.

It is the purpose of the writer to try to turn the minds of the people to a careful and prayerful consideration of the divine promises. It is to be deeply regretted that the clergymen would oppose an effort to teach the people the Bible truths; nevertheless, we find much opposition everywhere, and many clergymen will attempt to prevent the people from reading what is here written. We, therefore, assure the reader that we have no ulterior motive in putting out this message. It is not propaganda. There is no desire nor effort to induce the reader to join anything. The motive for this publication is wholly unselfish. The writer has but one desire and that is to induce the people to read and rely upon the divine promises and thus fix their hearts and minds in this hour of distress upon mankind; to comfort those that mourn and point them to a better day which is near at hand.

We should have in mind that the great, all-wise Creator has been nor for more titan 4,000 years dealing with certain people, preparatory to bringing to every man an opportunity for life everlasting. If he whose wisdom is perfect would devote so much time and energy to the outworking of a great plan, then surely it is worthy of the careful and painstaking examination and consideration of every man, without regard to his creed, religious training, or his political view.

Since the days of Abraham many men of unusual intellect not only have diligently studied the divine plan, but have devoted their lives to having a part in making it known to others. There were twenty-four holy prophets, whose messages are recorded in the Bible. All of these foretold a coming time of great blessings to the human race. Their utterances were not their own, but they spake as the spirit of Jehovah moved upon them. It was impossible for a human mind to look down through the corridors of the ages and to foretell what the future would bring forth; but these various prophets, guided by the all-wise Creator who knew the end from the beginning, wrote and spake merely as the instruments of God. God never failed in one of his promises. He says, "For I am the Lord, I change not".

(Malachi 3:6) "There hath not failed one word of all his good promise." (1 Kings 8: 56) All students of the Bible agree that the time must come when every promise of Jehovah will be fulfilled. Jehovah does everything orderly and on time and exactly in his own due time, and not man's due time. One day with him is as a thousand years and a thousand years as one day; and what might seem to man a long deferred fulfillment of a promise would be to God only a question of a very brief space of time.

All students of the Bible also agree that it has pleased Jehovah to divide the social order of things existing from the beginning of the world into epochs, which epochs we call worlds, and which the Lord speaks of as worlds -such a use of the word "world" meaning a social order of things existing within a given period of time. For nearly nineteen centuries students of divine prophecy have expected and looked for the world to end, because Jesus taught it would end. Many Christian men, however, failing to recognize the distinction between the symbolic and literal phrases of the Bible, have been confused concerning the end of the world. For instance, the great John Calvin taught that upon the happening of that event Jesus, reappearing near the earth, would cause fire to be emitted from the clouds, setting the earth aflame and totally destroying it and everything on it. He being a clergyman of great renown was supposed to have based his conclusions upon a proper interpretation of the Bible, and great numbers believed his teaching; and for this reason, with fear and trepidation, many have looked forward to the ending of the world.

Reason would lead us to the conclusion that Jehovah would not create a wonderful earth like this, permit man to bring it to a high state of cultivation in many places, and then completely destroy it. Such is wholly out of harmony with his character. Likewise such is wholly out of harmony with the plain teachings of his Word, which says: "The earth abideth forever". (Ecclesiastes 1:4) "For thus saith the Lord that created the heavens; God himself that formed the earth and made it; he hath established it, he created it not in vain, he formed it to be inhabited". (Isaiah 45:18) When the Bible speaks of the world ending it does not mean the literal earth, but it does refer to an epoch or dispensation of time during which a certain arrangement of things or social order exists. In proof of this the Scriptures disclose that there was a "world" which existed from the time of Eden until the great deluge: "Whereby the world that then was, being overflowed with water, perished". (2 Peter 3:6) At the end of the flood a new "world" began, and the promise is made by the same Scriptural writer that it shall end. The period of that world is from the flood until the coming of Messiah's kingdom, and his kingdom is to mark the beginning of another new world or new order of things. The first world, then, began with the creation of man and ended with the flood. At the time of the deluge began the second world, which the Scriptures speak of as "the present evil world; and God clearly foretold that the second world, or social order of things, visible and invisible, would pass away during a fiery time of trouble; and then would follow the world to come, the social order or arrangement of things. St. Paul instructs us to "rightly divide the word of truth"; and this means, amongst other things, to apply the texts of Scriptures within the period or epoch to which they belong; and applying these in their proper place, one can discern the orderly and majestic forward movement of the divine arrangement.

All students of the Bible further agree that just before Jesus was crucified he told his disciples that he was going away, but that he would return again and receive them unto himself, and that his second coming would mark the end of the world, i.e., the social order of things existing at the time he was on the earth. Other Scriptures show that at that time the great blessing long promised, viz., life, liberty and happiness, would be offered to the entire human family.

All students of divine prophecy agree that the promises of God made through the prophets must have a fulfillment some time, and that the time for fulfillment relating to the restoration of the human race to life, liberty and happiness has its beginning at the end of this world and at the beginning of the new world, i.e., at the time when the social order of things existing in Jesus' day shall pass away and the new order be established. By faith the prophets of old looked for that time and hailed its coming as the Golden Age, because during that age the Messiah shall reign and establish righteousness in the earth. It must be conceded, then, by all that the first important question for our determination is, When does this world end? If we can definitely fix this period, then it is an easy matter to determine when the divine promises with reference to life everlasting will be opened to the world in general. We therefore propose to prove in this argument that the social order of things, the second world, legally ended in 1914, and since that time has been and is passing away; that the new order of things is coming in to take its place; that within a definite period of time the old order will be completely eradicated and the new order in full sway; and that these things shall take place within the time of the present generation and that therefore there are millions of people now living on earth who will see them take place, to whom everlasting life will be offered and who, if they accept it upon the terms offered and obey those terms, will never die. If these facts can be established by competent testimony to the satisfaction of the reasonable mind, then every man should hail it with gladness, every one should be delighted, even though it upsets his preconceived opinions, formed from the study of the creeds and plans of men. We invite the reader, therefore, to examine each point carefully as here made, compare the argument with the Scriptures cited, and view the same in the light of present day events which are discernible to all eyes, and upon all this evidence reach a conclusion. Every man should be persuaded in his own mind and no man should permit himself to be deterred from examining a question based upon the Bible because a clergyman or any one else makes the unsupported assertion that it is dangerous or unworthy of consideration. Error always seeks the dark, while truth is always enhanced by the light. Error never desires to be investigated. Light always courts a thorough and complete investigation. Light and truth are synonymous. They are progressive, and "the path of the just is as the shining light, that shineth more and more unto the perfect day". (Proverbs 4:18) The Psalmist plainly tells us: "Thy word is a lamp unto my feet, and a light unto my path".-Psalm 119: 105.

Gentile Times

The term Gentile times as used in the Scriptures designates a period of time during which the Gentiles were to govern the peoples of earth. At the death of Jacob God organized Israel into a nation and dealt with that nation, to the exclusion of all other nations of earth, for a specific time. Time and again they departed from their covenant with Jehovah and he punished them. Time and again be warned them against a punishment of greater duration unless they profited by previous experiences. They had many kings -some good, some wicked. Zedekiah was the last king, and he became so very wicked that God issued this decree against him, saying: "Therefore thus saith the Lord God; Because ye have made your iniquity to be remembered, in that your transgressions are discovered, so that in all your doings your sins do appear; because, I say, that ye are come to remembrance, ye shall be taken with the hand. And thou, profane wicked prince of Israel, whose day is come, when iniquity shall have an end, thus saith the Lord God; Remove the diadem, and take off the crown: this shall not be the same: exalt him that is low, and abase him that is high. I will overturn, overturn, overturn, it; and it shall be no more, until he come whose night it is; and I will give it him." -Ezekiel 21:24-27.

It is a well-known historical fact that Zedekiah at the time here mentioned was taken prisoner by King Nebuchadnezzar and carried away to Babylon. Afterward the Israelites were permitted to maintain a national existence by other nations exercising a supervisory control oven them, and this condition continued until the year A. D. 73. What happened at the time of the dethronement of Zedekiah was that the crown, or dominion, or ruling authority oven the peoples of earth, was taken away from the Jews and permitted to be assumed by the Gentiles. The first universal empire was that of Babylon, followed by Medo-Persia, then by Greece, and later by Rome; and out of the Roman empire have grown all the Gentile nations of Christendom. As to how long this punishment should be inflicted upon the Jews, and therefore how long God would permit the Gentiles to have the dominion, is fixed by the Scriptures as seven symbolic times. (See Leviticus 26: 18) A time in the Scriptures is used to represent a symbolic year. According to the Jewish method of calculation a year is 360 days. A day for a year, then, would make each time 360 years in duration. The seven times would be a period of 2520 years, during which the Gentiles should have the lease of power, and at the end of which their lease of power would legally cease to exist.

The date of Zedekiah's overthrow and the establishment of Nebuchadnezzar's Gentile dominion, which was the first Gentile world government, is definitely fixed both by secular history and the Scriptures as B. C. 606. In the year A. D. 1, 606 years of the whole period had expired. Adding 1914 years to the 606 would make a total of 2520 years, therefore bringing the period of the Gentiles' lease of power or dominion to an end in the year 1914. This date corresponds with the circumstantial evidence proving conclusively when the world would begin to end, i.e., when the old order would begin to pass away, and fixes the time for the manifestation of Messianic power and the bringing in of the new order of things.

By way of illustration, if a man purchases a piece of property on which is situated a decayed building and upon which lot he expects shortly to erect a new structure, the first work in which the new owner engages is to clear the lot of the decayed building, preparatory to erecting the new. By analogy, then, if the old order began to pass away in 1914 and Messiah began to exercise his power, preparatory to setting up the kingdom of righteousness, then we should expect that his first work would be the destruction of the old systems of unrighteousness.

We here introduce the testimony of a witness whose competency cannot be questioned and whose testimony must be accepted as absolutely true. This witness is Jesus of Nazareth. To orthodox Jews he was a great teacher amongst the Jews. To Christians he was not only a great teacher, but by them is accepted and recognized as the Son of God, the Redeemer of mankind, the Savior of the world, the King of glory. He testified that the Jews should be trodden down of the Gentiles until the times of the Gentiles be fulfilled. {Luke 21:24) He gave to John the Revelator instruction as to what would take place when that time should arrive and when he, the Messiah, should begin to exercise his kingly power. He pictures the prophets, the mouthpieces of Jehovah, as saying concerning himself, the Messiah: "We give thanks, O Lord God Almighty, which art, and wast, and art to come; because thou hast taken to thee thy great power, and hast reigned [exercised regal authority]. And the nations were angry, and thy wrath is come."-Revelation 11:17, 18.

Here, then, we definitely see that the Gentile times ended in the fall of 1914. At that time, true to the prophetic statement, the nations did become angry and God's wrath has been upon the nations since. Every nation under the Sun has been growing weaker.

End of the World

Fully corroborative of this testimony, we direct attention to the further testimony of Jesus set forth in the 24th chapter of Matthew only a few days before his crucifixion, to wit, in the spring of A. D. 33: "As he sat upon the mount of Olives, the disciples came unto him privately, saying, Tell us, when shall these things be? and what shall be the sign of thy presence, and of the end of the world?" After giving them warning not to be deceived by other testimony, the Lord plainly answers their question: "Nation shall rise against nation and kingdom against kingdom; and there shall be famines, and pestilences, and earthquakes, in divers places. All these are the beginning of sorrows." (Matthew 24:7, 8) In other words, he stated that a great world war would ensue, in which the nations and kingdoms of the earth should be involved. That great war began exactly on time, at the end of the Gentile times; and there the old order began to pass away. The war, involving nearly all the nations of earth, continued for about four years, and its destructiveness of treasure and human life is unparalleled in any other time of man's history.

It will be noticed that Jesus said this would be accompanied by famine. Since the coming of the war there has been great distress in the world because of the shortage of food. In many of the countries of Europe thousands have literally starved to death. The food shortage in every country on earth is very apparent and the cost of living mounts higher and higher. This is not due to the fact that the earth is less productive, nor is it due to the fact of man's inability to plant and produce more; but it is due to the unsettled conditions resulting from the world war, which conditions Jesus clearly foretold would accompany the war; and it is another evidence that 1914 marked the beginning of the end of the world; for Jesus plainly said, "These are the beginning of sorrows".

Furthermore, it is observed, Jesus said that the war and famine would be accompanied by a pestilence. This has been literally fulfilled. The Spanish influenza swept over the earth and in less than twelve months the victims from that dread pestilential disease outnumbered two to one of those who died during the great world war in four years; and now this is being followed in the European countries by the direful pestilence of typhus, against which the people are being warned. Again Jesus said that the war, famine and pestilence would be followed by earthquakes. It was not unusual for Jesus to use symbolic language; in fact, he often used symbolic language or dark sayings to conceal the real meaning until the due time should come. In Biblical symbology earthquake means revolution. Following the war have come famine, pestilence and revolutions in many countries -some bloody and some bloodless. Russia has experienced her revolution and there the Babylonish systems have fallen. The same thing has occurred in Germany, in Austria and Hungary; and the spirit of revolution is rife everywhere. This does not mean the end of the trouble, but it does mean, according to Jesus' words, that the old world legally ended in 1914 and the process of removing the worn out systems is now progressing, preparatory to the inauguration of Messiah's kingdom.

Corroborative Testimony

It will be interesting here to examine a picture that Jehovah caused to be made centuries ago. The prophet Elijah was used as a type of the true followers of Christ Jesus. His journey to Mount Horeb pictures the journey of the true Christians down to the time of the end of the world. The Lord directed him to go forth and stand on the mountain, picturing the church in such a position as to obtain a clear vision of the events about to transpire and transpiring. To Elijah the Lord said: "Go forth, and stand upon the mount before the Lord. And, behold, the Lord passed by, and a great and strong wing rent the mountains [symbolically representing kingdoms], and brake in pieces the rocks [strong parts thereof] before the Lord; but the Lord was not in the wind [symbolic of war]: and after the wind an earthquake [symbolic of revolution]; but the Lord was not in the earthquake: and after the earthquake a fire [symbolic of greater troubles]; but the Lord was not in the fire: and after the fire a still small voice." - 1 Kings 19:11, 12.

In 1898 Pastor Russell, the greatest Bible student of modern times, commenting on the above Scripture, said:

'The four exhibitions of the Lord, given to Elijah, represent, we believe, four manifestations in which the Lord is about to reveal himself to mankind, the first three of which will prepare men for the final one, in which will come the desired blessing to all the families of the earth. These are

"(1) The mighty winds rending the very rocks. Blowing winds seem to be used in Scripture for wars. The wars, whose dark clouds have threatened the civilized world so ominously for the past thirty years, have been miraculously hindered to give opportunity for 'sealing' the Lord's consecrated people in their foreheads (intellectually) with the present truth. We are therefore to expect that when these winds of war shall be let lose, it will mean a cataclysm of warfare which shall divide kingdoms (mountains) - prefigured by the mighty wind shown to Elijah (1 Kings 19:11), which rent the rocks. But God's Kingdom will not follow the epoch of war; the world will not thus be made ready for the reign of Immanuel. No; a further lesson will be needed and will be given. It is represented in

"(2) An earthquake. Throughout the Scriptures an earthquake seems always to represent revolution; and it is not unreasonable to expect that an era of general warfare would so arouse the lower class of Europe and so discontent them with their lot (and especially with the conditions which would follow such a war) that revolution would be the next thing in order. (Revelation 16:18) But, severe though those revolutionary experiences will be to the world, they are not sufficient to prepare men to hear the voice of God. It will require

"(3) The fire from heaven - an epoch of divine judgments and chastisements upon a maddened but unconverted world, wild in anarchy, as other Scriptures show us. The results of their wars, revolutions and anarchy, in the failure of their schemes, will have a humbling effect, and will prepare mankind for God's revelation of himself in

"(4) The still small voice. Yes; he who spoke to the winds and the waves of the sea of Galilee will, in due time, 'speak peace to the peoples'. He will speak with authority, commanding the observance of his long neglected law of love. 'And whosoever will not hear that prophet shall be cut off from among the people.' - Acts 3:23"-The Finished Mystery.

Every close observer will witness that this prophecy has been partially fulfilled and is still in course of fulfillment.

Israel's Double

The Jewish people God used as a typical people. Their law foreshadowed better things to come in the future. (Hebrews 10:1) Keeping in mind that prophecy means history written in advance, i .e., that the divine mind foreknew from the beginning the end and caused the salient points to be recorded for the benefit of those living at the times when they should happen, let us now examine further the testimony of Jesus on this point. He said: "Now learn a parable of the fig tree; When his branch is yet tender, and putteth forth leaves, ye know that summer is nigh: so likewise ye, when ye shall see all these things, know that it is near, even at the doors". (Matthew 24:32, 33) The fig tree here is symbolic of the Jewish nation. We reach that conclusion from what Jesus himself said in cursing the fig tree a few days before he gave utterance to the words above quoted.-Matthew 21: 19, 20.

Jehovah, through Jeremiah his prophet, foretold to Israel that the climax of their punishment would come when he would drive them out of the land of Palestine into a strange country, where they would have to serve others and be oppressed for the same length of time that he has shown them his favor, the words of the prophet here being: "Therefore will I cast you out of this land into a land that ye know not, neither ye nor your fathers; and there shall ye serve other gods day and night; where I will not show you favor. Therefore, behold, the days come, saith the Lord, that it shall nor more be said, The Lord liveth, that brought up the children of Israel out of the land of Egypt; but, The Lord liveth, that brought up the children of Israel from the land of the north, and from all the lands whither he had driven them; and I will bring them again into their land that I gave unto their fathers. Behold, I will send for many fishers, saith the Lord, and they shall fish them; and after will I send for many hunters, and they shall hunt them from every mountain, and from every hill, and out of the holes of the rocks. For mine eyes are upon all their ways: they are not hid from my face, neither is their iniquity hid from mine eyes. And first I will recompense their iniquity and their sin double; because they have defiled my land, they have filled mine inheritance with the carcases of their detestable and abominable things." - Jeremiah 16:13-18.

Here it is to be seen that God not only foretold driving them out and punishing them, but that he would ultimately bring them back into Palestine; and the length of their punishment would be an exact double - a counterpart of duplication-of the time during which he has bestowed his favor upon them. "First I will recompense their iniquity and their sin double." The word double here means duplication or exact counterpart. If we can get the proper location of these time features, ascertain where the double began, we can very easily determine when God's favor should be due to return to the Jews and what relation that has to the budding of the fig tree, as above stated.

God is his own interpreter and will make plain his plan to those who study to understand it. Through the mouth of another prophet he gives us the key to the location of the very day of the beginning of this double. The prophet Zechariah records concerning Jerusalem these words: "Rejoice greatly, O daughter of Zion; shout, O daughter of Jerusalem; behold, thy king cometh unto thee: he is just, and having salvation; lowly, and riding upon an ass, and upon a colt the foal of an ass". "Turn you to the strong hold, ye prisoners of hope: even today do I declare that I will render double unto thee." (Zechariah 9:9, 12) This prophetic statement of the Lord must have a fulfillment at sole time and it is quite evident that its fulfillment would mark the date from which the double counts.

Prophecy Fulfilled

On the 10th day of Nisan, A. D. 33, corresponding practically with our month of April, Jesus of Nazareth rode into Jerusalem upon an ass and offered himself as king to the Jews. St. Matthew records the incident in the following words: "And when they drew nigh unto Jerusalem, and were come to Bethphage, unto the mount of Olives, then sent Jesus two disciples, saying unto them, Go into the village over against you, and straightway ye shall find an ass tied, and a colt with her: loose them, and bring them unto me. And if any man say ought unto you, ye shall say, The Lord hath need of them; and straightway he will send them. All this was done that it might be fulfilled which was spoken by the prophet, saying, Tell ye the daughter of Zion, Behold, thy King cometh unto thee, meek, and sitting upon an ass, and a colt the foal of an ass. And the disciples went, and did as Jesus commanded them, and brought the ass, and the colt, and put on them their clothes, and they set him thereon. And a very great multitude spread their garments in the way; others cut down branches from the trees, and strewed them in the way. And the multitudes that went before, and that followed, cried, saying, Hosanna to the Son of David: Blessed is he that cometh in the name of the Lord; Hosanna in the highest."-Matthew 21:1-9.

Here, then, is a positive statement of the fulfillment of Zechariah's prophecy, and the very day of it is fixed; and so the Lord said, "Today I declare that I will render the double unto thee". That very day, then, marked the middle point in the history of the Jews. It is exceedingly important, then, to find out how long they had been in God's favor. The death of Jacob, when he called his twelve sons before him and blessed them, is the beginning of the nation of Israel; therefore the date of the beginning of the favor upon Israel. From the death of Jacob until the 10th day of Nisan A. D. 33 was 1845 years. That is to say, on the 10th day of Nisan A. D. 33 the double began to count, and from that day Palestine began to disintegrate, the Jewish nation began to melt away; and exactly forty years from that date Palestine was completely depopulated. In other words, a period of forty years was occupied by Jehovah from the time he began to execute the double until Palestine was completely depopulated. As evidence of this, we cite the following historical accounts:

"It may be proper to mention also what things occurred that show the benignity of that all-gracious Providence, that had deferred their destruction for forty years after their crimes against Christ." (Eusebius' Ecclesiastical History) "On the 15th day of Nisan, i.e., of April, in the year 73 A. D., the first day of the Easter festival, the same day on which, according to tradition, the God of Israel had led his people out of Egyptian bondage into freedom, the last bulwark of Israel's liberty had fallen, and Israel was delivered into bondage." (Cornil's History of the People of Israel) "Masada attained great importance in the war with the Romans. . . With the fall of Masada the war carne to an end, on the l5th of Nisan, 73." (The Jewish Encyclopedia) "The capture of Masada, a Jewish fortress on the southwestern shores of the Dead Sea, put a termination to one of the fiercest struggles recorded in history (73 A. D.)." (Morrison's Jews Under Roman Rule) "Judea was not entirely subjugated; for three strong fortresses were still in arms: Herodium, Machaerus, and Masada...The heroes agreed to this proposal (of their leader Eleasar) even with enthusiasm, and on the first day of the great Feast of the Passover (A. D. 73), after slaying their own wives and children, they all perished on their own swords." (Graetz's History of the Jews, Vol. 2) "Eleasar accordingly persuaded all his people during that night to kill their wives and children and then themselves, but to burn all their treasures first. The next day the Romans found only 960 dead bodies, whilst but two women and five children hid themselves in caverns and were discovered. The Easter of the year 73, just seven years from the beginning of the great movement and forty years after Christ's crucifixion, saw this end of the whole tragedy." (Ewald's History of Israel, Vol. 7) The historian Josephus corroborates these dates.

Double Begins To End

The double began to count, as stated, in the spring of the year A. D. 33; and since the period of favor had been 1845 years, the period of punishment should likewise be 1845 years. Then adding 1845 years to A. D. 33 brings us to 1878; and on the latter date, if our calculations be correct, we should find, according to the parallel or double, that some time during the year 1878 there should be some marked beginning of God's favor returning to the Jew. In other words, here should begin the budding of the symbolic fig tree, which ought to be specially marked forty years later, viz., in 1918, if this parallel is carried out.

Favor Begins To Return

In the summer of 1878, exactly on time and when we should look for God's favor to return to the Jew, we find there transpired a certain event of the greatest importance that had happened to Jewry in more than 1800 years. I quote from the Jewish Encyclopedia, which is a recognized authority: "Russia, at war with Turkey, was successful, and by the treaty of San Stephano practically effaced Turkey from Europe. Lord Beaconsfield, a Jew, came into power in 1874. As Premier of Great Britain Beaconsfield sent the English fleet into the Dardanelles and brought Indian troops to Malta and made a demonstration against Russia. She yielded and agreed to a discussion of the whole affair at Berlin. Accordingly from June 13 to July 13, 1878, the Berlin Congress was held. Beaconsfield compelled Russia to greatly modify her treaty. Turkey was enfranchised and made independent, but upon condition that civil and religious rights be granted to the Jews. This had an important bearing on the history of the Jews."

Other authorities state that Beaconsfield presided at that Congress, wrote the treaty and was the leading factor. As you well know, his real name was D'Israeli, a thorough, full-blooded Jew, the first and only Jewish prime minister Great Britain has ever had. From that time on the favor of the Lord began to be shown again to the Jewish people. According to the parallel we should expect God's favor to increase toward the Jews from 1878, and should have some special climax in the year 1918.

Zionism

For many centuries there have been repeated efforts to destroy the Jews, all of which have failed. God never intended that they should be destroyed and they never shall be destroyed. Their persecutions have held them together as a people and increased their longing desire for a home in the land of their fathers. In dealing with his people God always raises up a man at the opportune moment and often the man who proves his faithfulness to the task imposed upon him dies a martyr to the cause. In times past Jehovah has proven his purpose of making the wrath of man to praise him, and every one who has suffered for a righteous cause will in due time receive a reward for his faithfulness to the principles of truth and righteousness.

In 1860 there was born in Budapest a Jewish child who grew to manhood's estate. Choosing first the law as a profession, he soon embraced journalism and forged to the front amongst the journalists and writers of the world. His heart was torn and bleeding because of the wicked and unjust persecution of his kinsmen, the Jewish people, which led to the formation in his mind of a scheme for their relief. In 1896 he gave expression to this scheme in his splendid paper, A Jewish State; and there many Jews of the world began to awaken to the fact that their cause had found a champion in this man. When first A Jewish State appeared, his office assistant wept, because he thought the author had lost his mind; but as the import of this paper was considered, it was hailed as a message of deliverance by many of the oppressed Jews of the world. He spent his life in the interest of the cause and his last words were: "Greet Palestine for me; I have given my life for my people."

Today the name Theodor Herzl is a household word amongst the Jews of earth and the time will come when the peoples of earth, Jew and Gentile, will recognize that Theodor Herzl was raised up at the opportune moment to give birth to Zionism, which is destined to succeed beyond the dreams of its originator.

Cause for Zionism

What was the inducing cause for the formation of Zionism? Was it due to the prosperity of the Jews? No, indeed. Let the beloved Herzl answer: "The scheme in question [Zionism] included the employment of an existent propelling force. Everything depends on our propelling force. And what is our propelling force? The miseries of the Jews."

If we find that God foreknew the condition of misery of the Jews and permitted it to prepare the Jews for the Zionistic movement in order that they might be turned back to their homeland, will not that strengthen faith in the promises of Jehovah concerning what will be the ultimate result? "And I will cause them to pass over with thy enemies into a land which thou knowest not; for a fire is kindled in my anger, over you shall it burn." "Therefore will I hurl you out of this land into the land of which ye had no knowledge, neither ye nor your fathers; and there shall ye serve other gods by day and by night; so that I will not grant you and favor. Behold, I will send for many fishermen, saith the Lord, and they shall fish them; and after that will I send for many hunters, and they shall hunt them from every mountain, and from every hill, and out of the clefts of the rocks." "And thou shalt become an astonishment, a proverb, and a byword, among all the nations whither the Lord will lead thee." - Jeremiah 15:14; 16:13, 16; 24:9; Deuteronomy 28:37.

Development of Zionism

Officially organized in 1897, Zionism has advanced year by year. The first congress held in Basle, Switzerland, in that year was attended by 206 delegates, only a handful of Jews: whereas today Zionism has its organization in every part of the world where there are Jews and there are some of them almost everywhere. Large sums of money have been raised and expended in the establishment of many agricultural settlements. Scientific methods have been employed in agriculture. Schools have been established, and the foundation of the great Hebrew University has been laid on the Mount of Olives. The organization of colonies is progressing. Jews are acquiring the land in Palestine and building houses; waste lands are being reclaimed and gradually the nation is rising.

Double Fulfilled

When Zionism was organized, among other things the first congress declared that its aim was and is the procuring of such government sanctions as are necessary in the achievement of the objects of Zionism. As above noted, the favor of God began to return to the Jews in 1878 and according to the prophetic double foretold by the Lord's prophets, forty years later, or in 1918, there should be some marked and special manifestation of God's favor toward the Jew. The Jewish year begins in the autumn; therefore November, 1917, would be in fact the beginning of 1918. In 1917 the Allied armies drove back the Turk and took possession of Palestine. On November 2, 1917, or about the second month of the Jewish year 1918, Great Britain officially recognized Zionism, as appears from the following:

"Foreign Office. Nov. 2nd, 1917.

"Dear Lord Rothschild:

"I have much pleasure in conveying to you on behalf of His Majesty's Government, the following declaration of sympathy with Jewish Zionist aspirations, which has been submitted to, and approved by, the Cabinet: "'His Majesty's Government view with favor the establishment in Palestine of a National Home for the Jewish people, and will use their best endeavors to facilitate the achievement of this object. it being clearly understood that nothing shall be done which may prejudice the civil and religious rights of existing non-Jewish communities in Palestine, or the rights and political status enjoyed by Jews in any other county. "I should be grateful if you would bring this declaration to the knowledge of the Zionist Federation.

"Yours sincerely,
"ARTHUR JAMES BALFOUR."

Within the year 1918 ten nations of earth, including Great Britain and the United States, gave official endorsement of the establishment of a Jewish homeland in Palestine. It was in the spring of 1918, about the anniversary of the deliverance of the children of Israel from Egypt, exactly forty years from the time when the favor began to return to the Jew, that a commission in charge of Dr. Chaim Weizmann, with full authority from the British Government, sailed from London to Palestine, clothed with authority to the establishment of a Jewish commonwealth in Palestine. Thus we see that the double was fulfilled exactly on time, as God had foretold through the mouth of his prophets.

Purpose of Zionism

The first Zionist congress, convened at the instance of the much beloved Theodor Herzl, made a clear declaration as to its purpose and that program has never been altered. The purpose is thus stated:

"Zionism aims to create a publicly secured, legally assured home for the Jewish people in Palestine.

"In order to attain this object, the Congress adopts the following means:

"(1) The promotion of the settlement in Palestine of Jewish agriculturists, handicraftsmen, industrialists, and men following professions.

"(2) The federation and association of entire Jewry by means of local and general institutions in conformity with the local laws.

"(3) The strengthening of Jewish sentiment and national consciousness.

"(4) The procuring of such government sanctions as are necessary for achieving the objects of Zionism."

Jews Rebuilding Palestine

The Jews are not only laying a foundation of a state in Palestine, but they are putting in operation great schemes for improving the country by means of rapid transit systems, systems of irrigation, the building of houses, establishing of schools, and a great university at Jerusalem, and many other things. We cite a few of these events that have appeared in the public press:

Special Bulletin No. 469, issued by the Zionist Organization of New York City, states that the average rainfall in Palestine is twenty-six inches, and that this water stored up in Palestine would be sufficient to support a population of 15,000,000 people. The present population is 600,000. It further states that from the spring sixteen miles south of Jerusalem great quantities of water are flowing into the city. The public press announces gigantic irrigation schemes which, if carried out, will supply all Palestine with an abundance of water for irrigation and other purposes.

The Zionist Bulletin, under date of February 25, 1929, says:

"One million seven hundred thousand eucalyptus and other kinds of forest trees are to be planted on an area of 21,125 dunams.

"In Merchavia 20,000 eucalyptus trees are to be planted, in connection with the sanitation of the settlement, on 200 dunams.

"In Kinereth and Daganiah 42,000 eucalyptus and other kinds of forest trees are to be planted on 175 dunams on the slopes of the mountain, the farm of Kinereth, the banks of the Jordan and the shores of Lake Kinereth.

"In Benschemen about 70,000 trees are to be planted on 230 dunams.

"In Hulda 425,000 trees are to be planted on 140 dunams.

"In Ber-Tobiah (Kastinie) 27,000 trees are to be planted on 380 dunams, apart from those already mentioned above.

"In the surrounding of the colony of Chederah 50,000 trees in all, mostly eucalyptus trees, are to be planted on 1,000 dunams."

A special bulletin dated March 1, 1920, says:

"Three thousand school children of Jerusalem, celebrating the Jewish Arbor Day recently, planted 500 trees in the suburbs of the Holy City, inaugurating the afforestation program of the Zionists to plant one million trees this year in Palestine, according to a report from the Zionist Commission in Jerusalem.

"During 1919, 369,000 trees were planted in the effort to restore Palestine's forests, wantonly destroyed by Turkish misrule and by the war. The afforestation of Palestine, because of its importance in the agricultural rejuvenation of the country and in providing lumber for construction work of the future, is considered one of the biggest reconstruction projects that the Zionists are attempting in the Holy Land."

Another special bulletin, under date of March 26, 1920, says:

"For ten years this struggle was kept up, entirely by Jewish labor. Today this once barren soil is covered with forests of olive and almond trees, 150,000 olive and 10,000 almond trees. Last year 100,000 pounds of almonds were sold, which together with the proceeds obtained from the sale of hides and wool from the extensive raising of cattle and sheep, produced a net profit of 15 par cent, on the original investment."

It is of the keenest interest to all thoughtful persons to note that these activities of the Zionists were foretold by God's prophet more than 2,500 years ago, who wrote: "I will open on naked mountain-peaks rivers, and in the midst of valleys fountains; I will change the wilderness into a pool of water, and the dry land into springs of water. I will place in the wilderness the cedar, the acacia, and the myrtle, and the oil-tree; I will set in the desert the fir-tree, the pine and the box-tree together; in order that they may see, and know and take (it to heart), and comprehend together, that the hand of the Lord hath done this, and the Holy One of Israel hath created it."-Isaiah 41:18-20, Leeser.

"They Shall Build Houses"

At the Zionist Executive Council held February 16, 1920, at London, Dr. Ruppin in the debate proposed the founding of a large society which should begin to build houses for workers as rapidly as possible. And even now in parts of Palestine houses are rapidly undergoing construction for the benefit of the constant flow of Jewish population returning to the land. Again we find that this is clearly in fulfillment of prophecy written long ago for the purpose of encouraging the Jews to have faith in the promises of the Lord. The houses now built are not in the interest of profiteers, nor will the owners be permitted to oppress those who live in them; but the owners shell live in them as their own homes, as the prophet of the Lord foretold: "They shall build houses, and inhabit them; and they shall plant vineyards, and eat the fruit of them. They shell not build, and another inhabit; they shall not plant, and another eat; for as the days of a tree are the days of my people, and mine elect shall long enjoy the work of their hands. They shall not labor in vain, nor bring forth for trouble; for they are the seed of the blessed of the Lord, and their offspring with them." - Isaiah 65:21-23.

Thus the testimony definitely establishes the fact that God's favor has returned to the Jew; that the parallel is fulfilled; that the fig tree is putting forth its leaves, according to the promise -all of which Jesus said would take place at the end of the world.

Events of Noah's Day

Jesus did not leave us to make a decision upon the happening of one event, but he enumerated several things that would transpire during the period when the world is ending. He stated that as it was in Noah's day, so would it be at the end of the world. "As the days of Noah were, so shall also the coming of the Son of man be. For as in the days that were before the flood they were eating and drinking, marrying and giving in marriage, until the day that Noah entered into the ark, and knew not until the flood carne, and took them all away; so shall also the coming of the Son of man be." - Matthew 24:37-39.

The first world ended with the flood. One hundred and twenty years before the flood God instructed Noah to prepare for it, that he might save himself, and to preach to the people concerning the approaching end. In Noah's day the people pursued their usual and customary course of action and were wholly indifferent and oblivious to the fact that the old order of things was about to pass away in a great flood. So likewise today the mass of humanity, pursuing its usual way, is wholly oblivious to and entirely ignorant of the great transition period we are now in.

In Noah's day while he was preaching to the people concerning the coming end of the world many scoffed at him, jeered him and mocked him, and thereby testified to their ignorance concerning the events that were about to occur. Mark the parallel in events now transpiring. Shortly after the capture of Palestine by the Allied armies a number of good ministers of the gospel met in London and issued the following manifesto, as appears from a London press report:

"The following manifesto was recently issued by a number of England's most noted ministers:

"'First-That the present crisis points toward the close of the times of the Gentiles.

"'Second-That the revelation of the Lord may ha expected at any moment, when he will be manifested as evidently as to his disciples on the evening of his resurrection.

"'Third-That the completed church will be translated, to be "forever with the Lord".

"'Fourth-That Israel will be restored to its own land in unbelief, and he afterward converted by the appearance of Christ on its behalf.

"'Fifth-That all human schemes of reconstruction must be subsidiary to the second coming of our Lord, because all nations will be subject to his rule.

"'Sixth-That under the reign of Christ there will be a further great effusion of the Holy Spirit on all flesh.

"'Seventh-That the truths embodied in this statement are of the utmost practical value in determining Christian character and action with reference to the pressing problems of the hour.

"'This remarkable statement was signed by A. C. Dixon and F. B. Mayer, Baptists; George Campbell Morgan and Alfred Byrd, Congregationalists; William Fuller Gouch, Presbyterian; H. Webb Peploe, J. Stuart Holden, Episcopalians; Dinsdale T. Young, Methodist.'"

These are well-known names, and are among the worlds greatest preachers. That these eminent men, of different denominations, should feel called upon to issue such a statement is of itself exceedingly significant.

It is to be regretted that the ministers above mentioned do not represent the sentiment of the majority of clergymen in the world. To all people who think, it is apparent that there are two classes of ministers in the world: the good and the bad, the honest and the dishonest, the faithful and the unfaithful.

This same rule applies to almost any profession. But amongst all the professions of the world, the man who occupies the position of a minister of the gospel is honored above all others from the divine standpoint, because he is supposed to deal with things pertaining to the Word of God. A faithful fulfillment of his commission, then, puts him in the honorable roll from God's viewpoint. On the other hand, a man who assumes the title of a minister of the gospel and who yields to the flattery of the world and for this reason disregards the plain teachings of the Bible and leads the people into error is himself a dishonor to the ministry and a menace to the welfare of humanity. No honest minister will take issue with me upon this point. Any one who insists that this is not true at once puts himself in the category of the bad class. Let each one, then, apply the measuring rod to himself and see which class he is in. And if he sees he is in the wrong one, he will if he is honest get into the right class as quickly as possible.

An enterprising newspaper man presented a copy of the foregoing manifesto to all the leading clergymen of one of the metropolitan cities of America; and their action is an illustration of how the majority have regarded the matter. Invariably they scoffed at the thoughts therein expressed; and many of them answered, "It is nonsense to talk about the world coming to an end. That event will not happen for 50,000 years or more. This war is like any other war and these troubles upon earth signify nothing."

For more than forty years Pastor Russell, a faithful, consecrated Christian, proclaimed to the people by word of mouth, through the public press and through his books, that 1914 would mark the end of the Gentile times; that the world would begin to end at that time, and that Messiah's kingdom would shortly follow. A few ministers here and there joined with him in the proclamation, but the majority of them scoffed at him and said all manner of evil against him because of his faithful proclamation of the message. The inspired witness of the Lord corroborated his statement that there would be scoffers at this time who would oppose the testimony divinely provided, saying: "There shall come in the last days scoffers, walking after their own lusts [selfish desires], and saying, Where is the promise [proof] of his coming? for since the fathers fell asleep, all things continue as they were from the beginning of creation. For this they willingly are ignorant of, that by the word of God...the heavens [invisible ruling powers] and the earth [social order of things], which are now, ...are kept in store, reserved unto fire [destructive trouble] against the day of judgment and perdition of ungodly men."-2 Peter 3:3-7.

The clear fulfillment of the above prophetic statement ought to be sufficient to convince any reasonable and thoughtful mind that we are now passing through the transition period from the old to the new order of things.

Concerning this same subject, the great Master further said: "The sun [shall] be darkened, and the moon shall not give her light, and the stars shall fall from heaven, and the powers of the heavens shall be shaken". (Matthew 24:29)

These dark sayings or symbolic words of Jesus, as shown in the light of other Scriptures, mean this: The Sun represents the gospel of Jesus Christ and him crucified, the philosophy of the great ransom sacrifice. The moon pictures or symbolizes the Mosaic law covenant arrangement, which foreshadowed the development of God's plan in both the Gospel and Millennial ages. And the stars symbolize exalted ones, teachers of the divine Word.

In fulfillment of this prophecy of the Lord everybody has witnessed during the past decade a great falling away of clergymen from the plain gospel of Christ Jesus and him crucified. In November, 1917, there assembled in Carnegie Hall, New York, ministers of the Jewish, Protestant and Catholic faiths, to discuss a common basis for action. In all that meeting the name of Jesus as the great Redeemer was not mentioned. There was a decided tendency to unite upon questions relating to civil or political affairs, but the great doctrines of the truth taught by the apostles and prophets became darkened and were ignored. One speaker at that convention said: "Here are three steps which we may take: (1) the preparation of a book of selections from the Bible by an interdenominational commission appointed by the legislature or by the Board of Regents for use in the schools; (2) the formulation of a plan for non-proselyting cooperation between the schools and the various denominations, to the end that every child may have its democratical and its religious instruction; (3) the granting of Regents' credits for serious work and Bible study outside of the schools." This plan was enthusiastically adopted. Another speaker, Dr. Finley, at that convention said, as appeared in the public press: "The time is come for Protestants, Catholics, Jew and Gentile, to cooperate to the end that every child may have an intimation at least of his moral and religious inheritance". As further evidence, the Interchurch World Movement has united in action but absolutely ignored the doctrines of the truth. Their statement, which appeared in a bulletin issued in January, 1920, says: "We believe the time is fully ripe for such unity of action on the part of united Protestantism that, without attempting to solve the problems arising from divergent and conscientiously held points of view on matters of doctrine and policy, the churches are ready for a common program of activity".

In other words, they are ignoring the great fundamental truths of Christianity foreshadowed by the typical sacrifices and made certain by the one great sacrifice of Jesus, the selection of the church and through the church the restoration of the world during the reign of Christ -clearly in fulfillment of the Master's words.

The stars, here representing the teachers of spiritual things, are pictured as falling; therefore representing that men who have claimed to teach the divine Word have fallen to the common level of ordinary world politics. As to the character of the Interchurch World Movement and showing that the purpose is not in harmony with the divine plan and that it is ignoring the plain purpose of Jesus and the apostles, we quote language recently uttered by some of the leading figures in it. Dr. J. Carnpbehl White, Associate General Secretary of the Movement, according to the public press recently said: "To carry out the new program of the cooperative churches it will require 100,000 new employed leaders during the next five years. They must be college graduates. An outlay of from $250,000,000 to $300,000,000 will be required to finance this program during 1920, and it is proposed to raise it during the week of April 25 to May 2; one-third of the money to be devoted to education, another third to Americanization and a third to reaching the billion persons in the non-Christian world. The world will be ruled by the forces of Christianity in twenty years."

This Interchurch World Movement is what its name really implies, to wit, the world moving the churches, or the churches moving in the way of the world. The movement is really organized in the interest of big business and political forces. As evidence of this we cite the following from the Interchurch Bulletin of recent date:

"George W. Wickersham, formerly United States attorney general, says in an interview that there is nothing incompatible between Christianity and modern business methods. A leading lay official of the Episcopal Church
declares that what the churches need more than anything else is a strong injection of business methods into their management.

"To the missionary China owes her expertness in printing, as well as cotton and fruit agriculture.

"Siam has become proficient in tanning leather through the scientific aid of missionaries.

"Brazil and India have increased the food production of their soils through the guidance of men of the missions.

"Japan is richer through the introduction of American fruit trees by the advance of agents of Christianity and progress.

"Natives of South Africa, formerly unemployed, now earn wages in sugar plantations and in the cultivation of cocoa beans, introduced by missionaries."

The Reverend David Carnegie in the Toronto Globe says:

"The Church, on this side of the Atlantic, at any rate, has taken sides with the employing and governing classes because of self-interest. She has been disloyal and faithless to the charge committed to her, but, in spite of all, she remains the one great avenue through which all that Christianity stands for is expressed. She alone has the spiritual message for the regeneration of industry.

"How can the Church discover and use the secret of her power? She has to discover that society and industry are inseparably linked together, that underlying both are fundamental principles of which she is the exponent." Why do men who claim to be ministers of the divine Word so dishonor the profession and link hands with big business and politics? The real reason is that they have lost their faith in God and in his Word, the Bible. They are seeking prestige and power from human sources and not divine approval. As evidence of this we quote from the Chicago Herald and Examiner of recent date:

"Methodist ministers were told yesterday that the theological schools of America are drifting away from the teachings of Christ, and that the Bible is no longer regarded by many preachers as the standard of faith.

"Dr. Henry Paul Sloan of the New Jersey annual conference of the Methodist Episcopal Church spoke at the ministers' meeting held at First Church, Clark and Washington streets, on the course of study required by the church for every minister. He said twenty-five annual conferences had sent a petition to the coming general conference to he held at Des Moines next May, demanding the course be revised.

"'Many Methodist ministers disbelieve some of the fundamental conceptions of Christianity and teach the higher criticism, which is destructive of the foundations of evangelical belief,' said the speaker."

Occasionally we find a minister of the gospel who has the courage to tell some of his brethren of the ministry the truth concerning the present condition. We quote the Reverend William Allan, as reported by the New York American:

"'One reason why there is so much cause for complaint about poor attendance at most churches is because the Lord is not among us. In too many cases Christ is on the outside seeking to get in, while we are proud of the large sums of money we are able to raise by our great mass movements, acting all the time as if silver and gold could take the place of spiritual power and the grace of God, both of which only come when the Lord is among us. When he is among us "it will be noised abroad that he is in the house" and the world will once more flock to the place where Jesus is. "'Oh, for a return of the old days, with the Lord in the midst of the assembly of his people, directing and dominating the manifold activities of the church!'"

It is gratifying to see now and then some Chrístian paper courageously telling the truth. In an article concerning the Interchurch World Movement, the Christian Leader of Cincinnati editorially says:

"Any effort to secure apparent unity in sentiment and organization apart from the doctrine of Christ is wholly unworthy of the indorsement of any one who professes to acknowledge the sovereignty of our Lord and Savior. Neither the unity for which he so fervently prayed, nor the organization which meets his approval, nor the spirit of his life, can be obtained by rejecting the doctrine of Christ. The spirit and life of the Christ can not be manifest in the individual or in the organization of individuals unless there first be the doctrine of Christ. All talk therefore about accomplishing a union la spirit and organization without appealing to all to obey the gospel of Christ, is a cheat, a fraud, a deception, a device of Satan to deceive the unwary. It is a conglomerate farcical union for the purpose, chiefly, to bring the church of Christ into a compromising position and thus break the force of the distinctive gospel which she preaches, or to make her so odious la the sight of all denominationalists for not uniting la the Movement that all will shun her."

Wall Street's Sunday Clothes

It will be interesting to note the names of some men mentioned in the public press as prominently connected with the Interchurch World Movement and the corporations in which these gentlemen are officially interested and the capital represented by the corporations. Under the name of each we mention the names of the corporations with which connected, opposite which are set the assets of the respective corporations, as far as known:

ALFRED E. MARLING

President, New York Chamber of Commerce

Horace 5. Ely & Co

Chairman, Board of Directors of Advisory Council of Real Estate Interests Associates Land Co.

Bond & Mortgage Guarantee Co.

President, Chamber of Commerce of the State of New York

Columbia Trust Co.	$121,100,000
Commercial Union Assurance Co.	1,607,578
Fifth Avenue Bank of New York	21,306,000
Fulton Trust Co. of New York	8,780,000
Hanover Fire Insurance Co.	5,840,184
Mutual Life Insurance Co. of New York	673,714,294
New York Life Insurance & Trust Co.	33,958,000
Sailor's Snug Harbor	

GEORGE W. WICKERSHAM

Law firm of Cadwalader, Wickersham & Taft

American Hawaiian Steamship Co.	$5,000,000

ALEXANDER R.NICOL

Agwi Oil Co.	
Agwi Pipe Lines Co.	
Agwi Refining Co.	
Atlantic Gulf & West Indies Steamship Lines	$39,754,800
Atlantic Gulf Oil Corporation	20,000,000
Carolina Terminal Co.	100,000
Clyde Steamship Co.	7,000,000
Clyde Steamship Terminal Co.	100,000
International Shipping Corporation	100,000
Mallory Steamship Co.	7,000,000
Mexican Navigation Co.	5,000,000
New York & Cuba Mail Steamship Co.	10,000,000
New York & Porto Rico Steamship Co. of New York	50,000
New York & Porto Rico Steamship Co. of Maine	5,000,000
San Antonio Co.	50,000
San Antonio Docking Co.	1,000
Santiago Terminal Co.	
Scandinavian Trust Co.	34,264,000

Seventy-Sixth Street Co.	
Southern Steamship Co.	90,000
Summit Estates Co.	
United States & Porto Rico Navigation Co.	2,000
Wilmington Terminal Co.	100,000

CLEVELAND H. DODGE

Phelps Dodge Corporation	$45,000,000
Alamogordo & Sacramento Mountain Ry	3,900,000
Alamogordo Lumbar Co.	740,000
American Brass Co.	15,000,000
Atlantic Mutual Insurance Co.	16,823,491
Burro Mountain Ry. Co.	400,000
Commercial Mining Co.	
Dawson Fuel Sales Co.	
Dawson Railway & Coal Co.	3,100,000
El Paso & Northeastern Co.	16,792,000
El Paso & Northeastern Railroad Co.	5,400,000
El Paso & Rock Island Ry	5,000,000
El Paso & Southeastern Co.	25,000,000
El Paso & Southwestern Railroad Co.	19,055,000
Golden Hill Corporation	
Morenci Southern Railway Co.	1,250,000
Nacozari Railroad Co.	1,000,000
National City Bank of New York	887,193,000
National City Co.	
New York Life Insurance & Trust Co.	33,958,000
North Star Mines Co.	2,500,000
Old Dominion Co. of Maine	7,426,775
Russell Sage Foundation	

FLEMING H. REVELL

Fleming H. Revell Co.

Board of Home Missions of the Presbyterian Church of the U.S.A.

Missionary Review Publishing Co.
New York Young Men's Christian Association
New York Life Insurance Co. $995,087,285
Northfield Schools
Wheaton College, Norton, Mass

JOHN D. ROCKEFELLER, JR.

Bureau of Social Hygiene
China Medical Board
Colorado Fuel & Iron Co. $76,262,200
University of Chicago
General Education Board
International Health Commission
Manhattan Railway Co. $60,000,000
Merchants Fire Assurance Corporation of New York 2,786,431
Rockefeller Foundation
Rockefeller Institute for Medical Research

Mr. John D. Rockefeller, Jr., 18 also listed in Who's Who in America, 1920, as "looking after his father's interests"-the well known John D. Rockefeller, with wealth once said to exceed a billion dollars. Since 1899 the son has been, off and on, director of the following in addition to the foregoing:

Chicago Terminal Transfer Railroad Co.
Delaware, Lackawanna & Western Railroad Co. $42,597,000
Lake Superior Consolidated Iron Mines<
New York Produce Exchange Safe Deposit and Storage Co.
American Linseed Co. 33,445,678
National City Bank of New York 887,193,000
Puget Sound Reduction Co.
United States Steel Corporation 1,452,229,769
Missouri Pacific Railway Co. 345,632,400
Federal Mining & Smelting Co. 18,000,000
Standard Oil Co. of New Jersey 98,338,300

From the Los Angeles Times we quote:

"In short, religion has decided to adopt the methods of big business and brilliant financial cooperation, whatever its other multitudinous differences may be. Our Christian pastors and masters tell us, vide the advertisements, that 'business associations, governments and the leaders of the great religious bodies have surveyed world conditions, and their verdicts all agree' that nothing but millions can buy salvation for a 'world torn with war'. And they are probably right, since that same world which we are told 'a great shaft of light has struck', boasts few humble carpenters and fishermen to renounce all worldly comforts - disciples to follow a possessionless Master today.

Those expensive advertisements teem with ironical truths. 'The least pretentious business concerns now train their sales forces: can the churches do less?' they demand. 'In America we must have Sunday School experts, Bible teachers, skilled fishers of men. How very far we have traveled from the simplicity of Jesus, from the Sermon on the Mount, from that sublime doctrine, free and gratis for all who cared to take. 'The realization of humanity's need for Christ at this time has followed with sudden, blinding brilliance, not unlike that which came to Saul of Tarsus,' we are told. But Sauls of Tarsus seem to be peculiarly rare. Rather are they forsaking the ministry on all sides because of the meager worldly reward entailed. Nothing but millions can lure them back, or create new Sauls. Our modern Sauls don't accrue without expert training and the promised reward of high salaries.

"Every item in those expensive advertisements is quite logical. One cannot take issue with a single assertion. They all rock of efficient promise, of indubit-able statements as to conditions and needed reforms. And yet, somehow, they leave us with a feeling of irony that Christianity should have come to such a pass. Perhaps it is the glaring omission of exhortation to our spiritual duty-only our financial duty is emphasized. We are not asked to each and every one of us constitute ourselves a personal missionary without pay. We are not asked to examine the condition of our own souls, our own lives, our own spiritual practices; we are only exhorted to pay for the religious education of others, the religious improvement of others. There are numerous paragraphs beginning, 'Your money will,' etc., explaining just how much other people's service it will buy. There are paragraphs referring to our 'duty', but they all appertain to providing the money for other people's duties. In fact, there is a general impression of buying ourselves off from personal duties other than money and, as the advertisements themselves declare, 'It were folly to think that money alone could carry Christianity forward; the main problem has always been leaders. 'We must continue to send out men and women who will carry the Christ-life into their businesses, their recreations, and their homes. Send other people out-you seem not necessarily to be those people yourselves. 'Unless you falter, a generation of trained Christian leaders will make your children bless your name, is another form of exhortation-our faltering strictly taking the form of failing with the shekels.

'They will raise their hundred millions,...but unless most of us take our Christianity more personally and individually, unless we recognize a few other requirements in ourselves besides furnishing the money, our deputed Christianity isn't going to do the world much good, and our financial credit won't cut much ice in heaven."

Wall Street with a Pious Face

Roger W. Babson, statistician-in-chief of Wall Street, in a letter dated January 27, 1920, and given limited circulation, says concerning the churches: "The value of our investments depends not on the strength of our banks, but rather upon the strength of our churches. The underpaid preachers of the nation are the men upon whom we really are depending rather than the well-paid lawyers, bankers and brokers. The religion of the community is really the bulwark of our investments. And when we consider that only 15% of the people hold securities of any kind and less than 3% hold enough to pay an income tax, the importance of the churches becomes even more evident.

"For our own sakes, for our children's sakes, for the nations sake, let us business men get behind the churches and their preachers! Never mind if they are not perfect, never mind if their theology is out of date. This only means that were they efficient they would do very much more. The safety of all we have is due to the churches, even in their present inefficient and inactive state. By all that we hold dear, let us from this very day give more time, money and thought to the churches of our city, for upon these the value of all we own ultimately depends!"

Again the money-changers are operating in the house of the Lord, and again seem appropriate the words of the Master: "It is written, My house is the house of prayer; but ye have made it a den of thieves." - Luke 19:45, 46.

A More Honorable Way

Of course "big business" will raise the required money because it thinks this necessary.

Do the people wish to trust their spiritual interests with a class of men whose god is gold?

Occasionally yet very rarely you will find some denominational minister who sees the subtlety of this movement and who has the courage to speak out. Dr. A. T. Peterson, an Illinois Baptist preacher, says: "It is a super-league of nations".

Dr. Conant, an evangelist, in a published discourse involving the Interchurch World Movement, says:

"Mergers are the order of the day in every time of human activity, and the latest and most menacing is the Interchurch World Movement. By this movement the whole Christian Church is being unconsciously merged into a great union church which will be headed by liberals [infidels, higher critics, evolutionists, opposers of the interests of both God and man] "'This movement is shot through and through with fundamental error. Our Lord tells us that the mission of the church is to preach the gospel to every creature -just that and nothing more. But the leaders in this movement tell us that the mission of the church is to 'establish a civilization, Christian in spirit and in passion, throughout the world'. Those two conceptions will not mix any more than oil and water will.

"And by their social service program they are seeking to capture the functions of the state, and are thus uniting church and state."

Gospel as a Witness

Jesus further stated as an evidence of the end of the world: "This gospel of the kingdom shall be preached in all the world for a witness unto all nations; and then shall the end come". -Matthew 24:14.

If the leaders of the Interchurch Word Movement claim that their purpose is the conversion of the world to Christianity, then we say to them that they are too late. They are not doing it the Lord's way. In the first place, they are not preaching the gospel of the kingdom. They frankly state they are ignoring the doctrinal truths of the gospel. In the second place, the preaching of the gospel of the kingdom is not for the purpose of converting the whole world, but for taking out from the world "a people for his name". (Acts 15:14) And thirdly, this has already been done and we are at the end of the old order and the new is coming in.

Distress and Perplexity

The conditions which have arisen in the world since 1914 are distressing and perplexing. All the rulers of earth are perplexed. The financiers are in perplexity; the business men are in perplexity; the people are in perplexity; and all are in distress. Why is this so, and what does it mean? Jesus further answered concerning the end of the world, and in proof of it, that there would be "upon the earth distress of nations, with perplexity; the sea [restless humanity] and the waves [organized radical movements] roaring; men's hearts failing them for fear and for looking after those things which are coming on the earth; for the powers of heaven shall be shaken". (Luke 21:25, 26) This is daily in course of fulfillment.

As a sample of how the rulers of earth view the matter, President Wilson, in his speech before Congress after the great war began, said:

"These are days of great perplexity, when a great cloud hangs over the greater part of the world. It seems as if great, blind, material forces have been released which had for long been held in leash and restraint."

Fear has taken hold of men in all walks of life. Selfishness seems to pervade every line of business. The landlord, feeling that he may not get another such chance to reap a harvest, increases the rent upon his tenant. The groceryman, the dealer in other foodstuffs, clothing, etc., seem to fear that another opportunity will not come and that now advantage must be taken of this opportunity to get all the money possible. The spirit of distrust exists everywhere. All of this is but in fulfillment of the words of Jesus.

Man's Desire

Amidst all of this trouble, sorrow and distress, there is a longing desire in the hearts of the people; and that desire is for life, liberty, and the pursuit of happiness. Almost every one would prefer to dwell in peace with loved ones and to avoid strife and controversy; but conditions seem to be such that man's difficulties are insurmountable. They cannot do what they would like. Seemingly there is an unseen force or power controlling them. And what is that power?

Demons Active

Again we refer to the fact that as it was in Noah's day, so shall it be at the end of the world. The Scriptures clearly teach that in Noah's day the world had been overrun by fallen angels. As set forth in the sixth chapter of Genesis. these had assumed the forms of men and, in violation of their obligation to Jehovah, had selected wives from amongst the human race, and there resulted an offspring which was wicked to the last degree, and the whole earth was filled with violence. God brought on the deluge. The Apostle Peter, answering as to what became of these demons, said: "God spared not the angels that sinned, but cast them down to tartarus, and delivered them into chains of darkness, to be reserved unto judgment". "Christ also hath once suffered for sins, the just for the unjust, that he might bring us to God, being put to death in the flesh, but quickened in the spirit; by which also he went and preached unto the spirits in prison; which sometime were disobedient, when once the longsuffering of God waited in the days of Noah, while the ark was a preparing." (2 Peter 2:4; 1 Peter 3:18-20) "The angels which kept not their first estate, but left their own habitation, he hath reserved in everlasting chains under darkness unto the judgment of the great day." -Jude 6.

These demons, restrained in the atmosphere about the earth, have had power to communicate with the living ones of the human race through the instrumentality of mediums. These matters are fully discussed in my book, "Talking With the Dead", and I do not here go into detail. I merely call attention to the fact that the clear inference to be drawn from the above texts is that when the end of the world is reached the demons would have greater power and would exercise that power over men. The Czar of Russia was constantly in communication with the demons through a medium whom he kept in the royal palace. Emperor William of Germany claimed to have an "inner ear" and averred the he heard "voices" from beyond and was guided largely by these. The course of the demons is that of wickedness, and without a doubt the great world war which started in 1914 was chiefly induced by the influence of these demons.

The Scriptures tell us of a great whirlwind that will be raised up from the coasts of the earth. (See Jeremiah 23:19; 25:32, 33; 30:23,24) A whirlwind is a symbol of a great war. The great war created an interest in spiritism such as the world has never known; and some of the leading minds of the world have become devotees of it and are proclaiming the spiritualistic doctrine to the confusion of mankind. These demons are otherwise described in the Scriptures as the "four winds"; and Jesus speaking through the Revelator, said: "I saw four angels standing on the four corners of the earth, holding the four winds of the earth, that the wind should not blow on the earth, nor on the sea, nor on any tree, . . . till we have sealed the servants of our God". (Revelation 7:1-3) These winds, or powers of the air, are not powers of natural air, but are the powers referred to by St. Paul when he speaks of the prince of the power of the air". (Ephesians 2:2) These demons are exercising power over the minds of the people, causing distress, discontent, restlessness, hatred, ill-will, malice, strife, and all kinds of controversy and trouble.

All of the elements, as the Lord foretold through the Apostle Peter, are thus melting away amidst fervent heat.-2 Peter 3:10.

Remedies-Human

What remedies do men offer to bring order out of chaos and establish peace and prosperity amongst the people? The financiers desperately struggle to hold the present financial systems in order; but they have no remedy and know of none to bring about a better condition.

After centuries of effort, political parties have proved their inadequacy to meet the present conditions and to solve the distressing problems. Economists and statesmen, studying the question diligently, find that they are able to do nothing. and this applies to all political parties and organizations, for the reason that all are composed of selfish, imperfect men; and therefore cannot bring about an ideal condition.

League of Nations

With the cessation of hostilities, statesmen representing the leading nations involved met in conference and (giving them credit for the desire to establish peace and prosperity) the result of their deliberations was a covenant known as the League of Nations. This is offered as a remedy for present evils. Will it succeed? A league formed amongst all the nations of earth and based upon the principles of justice and righteousness, and in which all the contracting parties would honestly carry out the purpose expressed, would doubtless result in great good. But where selfishness is the chief motive and controls the action of any or all, an ideal condition could not be attained. God in his wisdom foreknew and foretold the formation of the League of Nations; and he likewise foretold that it must fail. -Isaiah 8:9, 10.

The inducing cause for the formation of the League is admittedly fear. Faith in God and his promises is entirely ignored. Because of these facts the League will never accomplish the expressed desire. It is not God's way. He has plainly said: "My thoughts are not your thoughts, neither are your ways my ways, saith the Lord. For as the heavens are higher than the earth, so are my ways higher than your ways, and my thoughts than your thoughts." (Isaiah 55:8, 9) Jehovah's great plan was entirely ignored in the formation of this League of Nations. The prophet truly wrote: "Blessed is the nation whose God is the Lord". (Psalm 33:12) But a nation that ignores the divine plan, or any league of nations formed which ignores the same, need not expect a desirable result. The Lord's prophet clearly had in mind the formation of the League of Nations, and also the league of ecclesiastical systems, when he wrote: "Associate yourselves, O ye people, and ye shall be broken in pieces: and give ear, all ye of far countries; gird yourselves, and ye shall be broken in pieces; gird yourselves, and ye shall be broken in pieces. Take counsel together, and it shall come to nought: speak the word, and it shall not stand." - Isaiah 8:9, 10.

Ecclesiastical Remedy

Ecclesiasticism relates to organized church systems, and particularly to the clergymen or priestly class operating and controlling the same. For a long time the Roman Catholic was practically the only creed extant. In the sixteenth century there was a great reformation movement and Protestant ecclesiasticism resulted. The ecclesiastics, therefore, come forward with a proposed remedy for distressed humanity; and since they do so, we are justified in a candid examination of their proposed remedy to see whether or not it is adequate. The ecclesiastical systems both Catholic and Protestant claim that their mission is to convert the world, thereby bringing the people into the churches. Let us suppose they could accomplish this expressed purpose and that the whole human race was brought into one or the other of the churches. What, then, is the hope that they hold out to the people?

The Catholic creed or teaching is that the destiny of man is fixed at death and that those who are good and faithful Catholics at death pass on to heaven, a condition of endless bliss. All other Catholics who have not been faithful in every particular go to purgatory, there to remain for an indefinite period of time (not less than a thousand years), during which time they are supposed to be cleansed and purified and made ready for the heavenly realm, that all the others, the heretics, the apostate, etc., must spend their destiny in hell fire, consciously suffering forever.

The Protestant teaching generally is that the destiny of every man is eternally fixed at death, the faithful church member passing at death into glory, a condition of bliss in heaven; and all others spending their eternity in conscious torture, eternal in duration.

It will be noticed, therefore, that if there be any real difference between these two remedies, the Protestant remedy is the worse of the two, because it offers no middle ground. It is plainly to be seen by any one that neither the Catholic nor the Protestant creed offers any remedy whatsoever for the present disorder that would lead to peace, prosperity, liberty and happiness and life everlasting on the earth. It follows, then, that if they should succeed in converting most or all of the people to their theories it would be no solution of the present problems.

The great difficulty with the systems ecclesiastical is that they ignore entirely the divine remedy. They ignore the commission given to the Christian and build their hopes upon manmade theories, creeds and institutions. They ignore completely the commission divinely given to every one who has consecrated himself to do the Lord's will. It will be admitted by both Catholics and Protestants that only a small portion of the earth's population have even pretended to embrace the teachings of their respective systems, and the most sanguine amongst them will never claim that they hope to convert everybody to their way of thinking and bring them into the church organization. The facts are that in modern times they have ignored the doctrines and do not ask the people to believe these but to unite in action; and the chief action is the solicitation and collection of money. Seizing the war spirit, the spirit of the world, these ecclesiastical systems now are engaged in raising millions of dollars, saying to the people: "If only we had the money we could convert the world". Is it not apparent to all that this is a reflection on the Lord, that he needs money to carry out his purposes; and is he pleased to use the unconsecrated funds of the worldings to do his work? Is it necessary to solicit in the name of the Lord money from men who have no interest in the Lord's arrangement but who yield to the importunities of the clergy and pay the money in order that they may have a social or political standing amongst a certain class of people? Could it be said that the Lord must resort to such methods in order to carry out his arrangement? Every reasonable man must say, Surely not. And again we are reminded of the Lord's words through the prophet, directing them at those who are advancing these worldly theories: "My thoughts are not your thoughts, neither are your ways my ways, saith the Lord. For as the heavens are higher than the earth, so are my ways higher than your ways, and my thoughts than your thoughts."-Isaiah 55:8, 9.

The wise man, then, is he who seeks to know what is the divine remedy and, finding this, seeks to conform himself to it; for nothing else short of divine power can bring order out of the present chaotic condition and bring to man that which he desires. Let us keep in mind that it has ever been the desire of man to enjoy life, liberty and happiness. This was so uppermost in the minds of the forefathers in laying the foundation for the American government that they placed this statement in the fundamental law of the land. The people, therefore, are wasting their money, wasting their time and energy to pursue a will-o'-the-wisp, a man-made theory, in utter disregard of the divine remedy; and, of course, if the people are ignorant of this remedy which the Lord has provided, they cannot pursue it.

The great masses are ignorant and their ignorance is due to the fact that the ecclesiastics have been unfaithful to their commission, have failed to teach the Scriptures, but on the contrary have taught man-made theories; and for this reason God, foreknowing that it would be thus, recorded: "Behold, the days come, saith the Lord God, that I will send a famine in the land, not a famine of bread, nor a thirst for water, but of hearing the words of the Lord. "-Amos 8:11. After many centuries of divine favor the clergy of the church nominal as a class has proven unfaithful to the divinely given commission. After six thousand years of laborious effort to establish an ideal government in the earth, the nations are now face to face with a condition of chaos, and mankind is groping blindly about. The people who love righteousness and truth have been without aid, advice and comfort from those from whom they might expect it and who claim to be the messengers of the Lord. These so-called spiritual advisers have torn off the mask and now boldly declare that they ignore the doctrines and unite in action for money and power.

With the great doctrines of Christianity ignored, upon what will the hungry souls feed? -those souls that hunger and thirst for righteousness, from whence will they gather their satisfying portion? (Psalm 107:1-7) Is it not time for all such to seek the divine remedy? Man's extremity is God's opportunity. The whole world is being humbled by suffering and sorrow. Let those who mourn be comforted by the great and beneficent arrangement disclosed by his Word.

Remedy-Divine

The Holy Scriptures contain the expression of the will of God concerning man. The Bible is the only true source of knowledge upon which man can base a hope for the future. The Apostle Paul with prophetic vision, looking on down to the time of the blessings that shall come to the human race, wrote to the followers of Jesus: 'Eye hath not seen, nor ear heard, neither have entered into the heart of man, the things which God hath prepared for them that love him. But God hath revealed them unto us by his spirit: for the spirit searcheth all things, yea, the deep things of God.' - 1 Corinthians 2:9,10. It was the great Master who said: "Sanctify them through thy truth: thy word is truth". (John 17:17) Nothing, then, but an understanding and appreciation of the Word of God can lead man into the right way and unfold to him visions of the blessings that are to come; and the understanding of the divine arrangement brings comfort and joy to the heart.

The inspired witness wrote: "Known unto God are all his works from the beginning of the world". (Acts 15:18) From the very creation of man to the full consummation of his plan Jehovah knew everything and his great program has been working out in a progressive and orderly manner. In order, therefore, for us to appreciate the divine remedy we must first ascertain the real cause of the present condition of strife, turmoil, trouble, wars, revolution, etc., in the earth.

The Cause

The first man was created perfect and given a perfect home in Eden, endowed with life as a human being, with happiness, with peace, and with all the blessings incident to a perfect life and a perfect home. He was endowed with the power and authority to produce perfect children and to fill the earth with a perfect race of people. His enjoyment of those blessings eternally depended upon his obedience to the divine law; and his disobedience of that law he was informed would lead to the forfeiture of his right to life as a human being, as well as his right to happiness and peace. Man violated the law. This account is briefly set forth in the third chapter of Genesis. Man was sentenced to death, driven out from his perfect home, and the judgment executed by causing him to subsist upon the poisonous elements of the unfinished earth. As long as he existed he was caused to eat his bread in sorrow. In all these centuries he has been under the bondage of the evil effects of sin, waiting and hoping for liberation.

It must be observed that Adam did not lose a home in heaven. He was not offered a home in heaven; but what he did possess was a home on earth, with human life in perfection, as a man; and his violation of the law forfeited these. Therefore, if man is ever restored to his original favors and blessing it must be to that which he first enjoyed -perfection of life as a human being, a perfect home, and peace and happiness on earth.

The disobedience of Adam entailed upon all of his offspring sorrow, sickness, suffering and death. The perfect pair did not bear children while in Eden; but they exercised this function after the condemnation and after man was earning his bread in the unfinished earth. He was gradually undergoing the sentence of death. He was imperfect, and it follows as a logical and reasonable conclusion that he could not produce a perfect race of people. The result was that his offspring were born in a dying condition. And this is what the prophet meant when he wrote: "Behold, I was shapen in iniquity; and in sin did my mother conceive me. (Psalm 51:5) This is the same thought expressed by St. Paul when he wrote: "Wherefore, as by one man sin entered into the world, and death by sin; and so death passed upon all men for that all have sinned". -Romans 5:12.

Redemption Promised

Jehovah had in mind from the beginning the redemption of mankind from this condition of suffering and death, and their restoration to that which was lost. Abraham, who lived in the land of the Chaldees, trusted in Jehovah; and God called unto him and made him a promise. saying: "I will bless thee, and make thy name great; and thou shall be a blessing: ...and in thee shall all families of the earth be blessed". (Genesis 12:2, 3) At the time this promise was made Abraham had no children. He was seventy-five years of age, his wife had passed the age of child-bearing; yet he had faith in God, and when Abraham was a hundred years old his son Isaac was born. When Isaac grew to manhood's estate God put Abraham to a test of faithfulness to him and directed Abraham to take his son Isaac into a mountain and offer him up as a sacrifice. It grieved Abraham's heart much to do this; but having faith in God he obeyed. Journeying to the mountain, he built an altar, bound Isaac to it, and the knife in his hand was about to strike death to his son when the Lord called unto him out of heaven, saying: "Lay not thine hand upon the lad, neither do thou any thing unto him: for now I know that thou fearest God, seeing thou hast not withheld thy son, thine only son, from me". (Genesis 22:12) There-upon God renewed his promise to Abraham and bound it with his oath, saying: "By myself have I sworn, saith the Lord, for because thou hast done this thing, and hast not withheld thy son, thine only son: that in blessing I will bless thee, and in multiplying I will multiply thy seed as the stars of the heaven, and as the sand which is upon the sea shore; and thy seed shall possess the gate of his enemies; and in thy seed shall alt the nations of the earth be blessed; because thou hast obeyed my voice".-Genesis 22:16-18.

This promise to Abraham has not yet been fulfilled. It must be fulfilled, because God is not slack in any of his promises. He changes not. (Malachi 3:6) Clearly, the blessing here intended is life, liberty and happiness-a restoration to the very things Adam had forfeited by reason of his disobedience. All the prophets who thereafter wrote foretold the coming of such times of restoration and blessing.

The judgment of condemnation against Adam could never be reversed because that would be equivalent to God denying himself; therefore the judgment must be enforced. But it would be entirely consistent with the divine arrangement for provision to be made for satisfaction of the judgment, thus maintaining the dignity and majesty of the divine law. Hence God made promise through the prophet Hosea, saying: "I will ransom them from the power of the grave; I will redeem them from death: O death, I will be thy plagues; O grave, I will be thy destruction".-Hosea 13:14.

This provision for the satisfaction of justice and release of mankind from condemnation must come through the voluntary sacrifice of another perfect human. The word ransom means exact corresponding price. A perfect man had sinned and forfeited life, liberty and happiness. This penalty was demanded by the divine law. Hence God could make provision and did make provision that if another perfect man could be found who would voluntarily permit his life, liberty and happiness to be taken from him, all these rights could be substituted for those which Adam had forfeited and thereby lay the foundation or basis upon which Jehovah could restore Adam and his offspring to liberty, happiness and life. Of course, it follows that none of Adam's offspring could meet these divine requirements, for the reason that all are imperfect. Hence the Psalmist wrote: "None of them can by any means redeem his brother, nor give to God a ransom for him". (Psalm 49:7) What, then, could be done for the redemption of the human race?

The Ransomer

St. John records the fact that the Word or Logos was the beginning of Jehovah's creation, and that he (the Logos) afterward became the active agent in the creation of everything made; and that "the Word [Logos] was made flesh, and dwelt among us, and we beheld his glory, the glory as of the only begotten of the Father, full of grace and truth". (John 1:14) St. Matthew gives the account of the birth of Jesus; that he was begotten not by man but by the power of Jehovah; therefore he had none of the inherited condemnation of contamination of Adam. The Logos was transferred from the spirit to the human plane. He became the child Jesus. He was born "holy, harmless, undefiled, separate from sinners" (Hebrews 7:26); he was without sin. (1 Peter 1:19) He was born under the law covenant, which covenant fixed the legal majority for priestly purposes at thirty years. Therefore when Jesus attained the years of maturity he was perfect physically, mentally, morally -perfect under the law, the exact counterpart of the perfect man Adam in Eden prior to his disobedience to the divine law. Why had Jehovah permitted his beloved Son to be transferred from the spirit to the human plane? Why had he come to earth at all? Let Jesus himself answer: "The Son of man came not to be ministered unto, but to minister, and to give his life a ransom for many". (Matthew 20:28) And again he said: "I am come that they might have life, and that they might have it more abundantly". (John 10:10) Again, speaking in dark saying or symbolic phrase, he likens himself unto bread, which men eat and live, saying: "I am the living bread which carne down from heaven: if any man eat of this bread, he shall live for ever; and the bread that I will give is my flesh [humanity], which I will give for the life of the world". - John 6:51.

The Ransom Price

To ransom means to purchase, and the ransom price means the exact corresponding price. A perfect man had sinned and lost all. A perfect man now, by voluntarily going into death, would provide the corresponding price for the redemption of mankind. Jesus was not a sinner. He never committed a sin. Why, then, should he die? St. Paul answers: "Christ died for our sins according to the Scriptures". (1 Corinthians 15:3) St. John adds: "He is the propitiation [satisfaction] for our sins: and not for ours only, but also for the sins of the whole world".-1 John 2:2. "God so loved the world, that he gave his only begotten Son, that whosoever believeth in him should not perish, but have everlasting life. For God sent not his Son into the world to condemn the world; but that the world through him might be saved." (John 3:16, 17) Jesus was put to death in the flesh, a man, and was raised from the dead a spirit being, divine in nature. (1 Peter 3:18) He ascended on high as a divine being, having the right to a perfect human life, now to be given in the place of that which Adam had forfeited; and by this perfect human life and all the rights incident thereto he had provided the ransom or purchase price for the redemption and deliverance of all mankind from death. As surely as God has made this provision, so surely then he will carry it into full force and effect.

The Seed

It will be noticed that in the promise God made to Abraham he said: "In thy seed shall all the families of the earth be blessed". (Genesis 28:14) The blessings here promised is life everlasting. (Romans 6:23) It follows, then, that before the blessing of life everlasting and the blessings incident thereto could be extended to mankind through the seed, the seed itself must first be developed. The seed according to the promise was the mystery for ages and generations. It is yet a mystery to all except those who have given their hearts to the Lord and diligently sought to understand what constitutes the seed. The Apostle Paul under inspiration defined the seed: "Now to Abraham and his seed were the promises made. He saith not, And to seeds, as of many; but as of one, And to thy seed, which is Christ." (Galatians 3:16) The word Christ here means anointed one. The word Messiah means the same thing. The Christ consists of Jesus glorified, the head, and the members of his body, which constitutes the church. "For as many of you as have been baptized into Christ have put on Christ. And if ye be Christ's, then are ye Abraham's seed, and heirs according to the promise." (Galatians 3:27, 29) "And he is the head of the body, the church: who is the beginning, the firstborn from the dead; that in all things he might have the pre-eminence."-Colossians 1:18.

Selection of Body Members

Clergymen as a class, particularly of modern times, seem to misconceive entirely the commission of a Christian and the purpose that God has in developing that class. They have conceived the thought and advance it to the people that everybody must join some denominational system in order to be saved; whereas the Scriptures plainly teach that God's purpose and plan, during the time elapsing from the crucifixion of the Lord to the setting up of his kingdom, is to select from amongst men his church. The word church means called-out class. It does not mean any denominational system. It means the true followers of the Master who continue faithful unto death. The Apostle Paul speaks of the church when he refers to the "church of the firstborn, which are written in heaven". (Hebrews 12:23) He does not say, Whose names are written on church books, or who have signed pledges to contribute so much money - not the names of those who are recorded by men, but who are recorded by the Lord in heavenly records, based upon their consecration and faithful service to him. The divine purpose is clearly set forth: "God at the first did visit the Gentiles, to take out of them a people for his name. And to this agree the words of the prophets; as it is written, After this I will return, and will build again the tabernacle of David, which is fallen down; and I will build again the ruins thereof, and I will set it up; that the residue of men might seek after the Lord, and al the Gentiles, upon whom my name is called, saith the Lord, who doeth all these things."-Acts 15:14-17. In the Scriptures a pure virgin is used to symbolize the bride of Christ, the true church; and an unchaste woman, or harlot, is used to symbolize the false system; and the Lord showed that these two would be in development side by side and that the pure virgin class would be persecuted by the unchaste class. The Lord Jesus gave a parable, likening these two classes unto wheat and tares, the true church being designated as wheat, whereas the others are designated as tares. (Matthew 13:24-39) He said: "Let us both grow together until the harvest: and in the Lime of harvest I will say to the reapers, Gather ye together first the tares, and bind them in bundles to burn them: but gather the wheat into my barn". The great apostate systems are binding themselves together in bundles and the Lord is gathering his true saints unto himself. Defining this parable Jesus said: "The good seed are the children of the kingdom; but the tares are the children of the wicked one; the enemy that sowed them is the devil; the harvest is the end of the world". (Matthew 13:38, 39) Further answering the question as to what would happen at the end of the world, he said he would send forth his messengers with the "sound of a trumpet [proclamation of the truth], and they shall gather together his elect from the four winds, from one end of heaven [ecclesiastical systems] to the other". (Matthew 24:31) For the past forty years or more the true Christians have been gathering themselves together without regard to creed or denomination, while the denominational systems are binding themselves into great compacts or leagues, and making much fuss about converting the world.

A Christian's Tribulation

It has become a popular matter to become a member of some church system or to join the Interchurch World Movement; and the man or woman who contributes the greatest amount of money is the one who receives the greatest honor. On the contrary, it has never been popular to be a true Christian, a true follower of Jesus; and this is due to the fact that the divine program is: "We must through much tribulation enter into the kingdom of God". (Acts 14:22) Jesus said: "If any man will come after me, let him deny himself, and take up his cross, and follow me". (Matthew 16:24) Jesus consecrated himself fully to do the Father's will. His footstep followers must do likewise. Jesus suffered indignities and persecution at the hands of the religionists of his time. His followers must have a similar experience. "For even hereunto were ye called: because Christ also suffered for us, leaving us an example, that ye should follow his steps." (1 Peter 2:21) Jesus said: "The disciple is not above his master, nor the servant above his lord. It is enough for the disciple to be as his master, and the servant as his lord. If they have called the master of the house Beelzebub, how much more shall they cal them of his household?" (Matthew 10:24, 25) Again he said to his followers: "If the world hate you, ye know that it hated me before it hated you. If ye were of the world, the world would love his own; but because ye are not of the world, but I have chosen you out of the world, therefore the world hateth you. Remember the word that I said unto you, The servant is not greater than his lord. If they have persecuted me, they will also persecute you; if they have kept my saving, they will keep yours also." (John 15:18-20) Suffering ignominy and persecution at the hands of the nominal religionists and the forces that they can bring to bear, is the course clearly marked out for the true follower of Christ Jesus. "The Spirit itself beareth witness with our spirit, that we are the children of God; and if children, then heirs; heirs of God, and joint-heirs with Christ; if so be that we suffer with him, that we may be also glorified together." (Romans 8:16, 17) "It is a faithful saying: For if we be dead with him, we shall also live with him: If we suffer, we shall also reign with him."-2 Timothy 2:11, 12.

The divine arrangement makes it a condition precedent to entering into glory that the true Christian should be perfected through suffering. The church is but a small number, comparatively speaking; and the church, together with Christ Jesus, the head, is called to the high and exalted position in heaven, constituting the seed of Abraham according to the promise, pictured by the stars mentioned in the promise. Hence, because of this exaltation, God permits them to be put through a period of trying circumstances and sufferings in order that they might be afforded the opportunity of proving their faithful, loyal devotion to him. "For it became him, for whom are all things, and by whom are all things, in bringing many Sons unto glory, to make the captain of their salvation perfect through sufferings. For both he that sanctifieth and they who are sanctified are all of one: for which cause he is not ashamed to call them brethren."-Hebrews 2:10,11.

True to the divine arrangement, the church has been put through a course of suffering. The head and the body members have been unjustly accused of crime time and again. St. Paul tells us, as likewise does the Master, that Satan is the god of this world. (2 Corinthians 4:4) Again we read that the whole world lieth in the wicked one. (1 John 5:19) The governments of earth, therefore, have been under the dominion of Satan, and the seed of Satan is and has been the instrumentality he has used for the purpose of persecution. In the days of the Master the scribes, Pharisees, and doctors of the law, who claimed to sit in Moses' seat and represent Jehovah, were the ones who led the persecution against the Master. Jesus plainly told these that they were a part of the seed of the serpent, the devil. It would be most reasonable, therefore, to expect that Satan would inject into the minds of his instruments the thought of charging the followers of Jesus with the crime of sedition against his (Satan's) empire. The nominal religionists of his day charged Jesus with the crime of sedition and caused him to be executed on that charge. St. Stephen, the first martyr to the cause of true Christianity following the Master, was stoned to death after being unjustly convicted upon perjured testimony on the charge of sedition. St. Paul, because of his faithfulness to the Lord, was confined in prison for four years under a similar charge and was otherwise ill-treated. St. John the Revelator, under a similar charge, was banished to the isle of Patmos and required to don a prisoner's garb and beat rock. The history of the world shows that the true followers of Jesus have met with opposition and persecution upon all hands and at all times.

As an illustration of this fact: the church nominal of England became a part of the political power and those who refused to conform to the state-church were persecuted. A short distance from London stands a building erected to the memory of men who were burned upon that spot because of their faithfulness to the truth and who refused to conform to man-made theories of religion. John Bunyan, a humble follower of Jesus, refused to be a conformist to man-made theories and he was tried and convicted and placed in prison. A clergyman then was delegated to wait upon him and tell Bunyan words to this effect: You are going to be kept in prison for three months. If at the end of that time you recant and conform yourself to the church-state you will be released; otherwise you will be put to death. And Bunyan calmly replied: "You might as well put me to death now; I will never conform". He was kept in prison for twelve years and while there wrote Bunyan's Pilgrim's Progress, which has been a great comfort and help to Christians who have trod the narrow way from then until now.

Speaking of the evidences concerning the end of the world, Jesus furthermore said: "Then shall they deliver you [meaning his followers] up to be afflicted, and shall kill you: and ye shall be hated of all nations for my name's sake". -Matthew 24:9.

It is often true that advantage is taken of conditions of war and strife to vent some ill-feeling upon others. When the great world war began, in Germany certain Christians, known as Bible Students, who asked to be exempted from combatant military service because of their devotion and faithfulness to the Lord and because of his command to them that they should not kill, were ill-treated, placed in the front ranks of battle, and were amongst the first to fall. In Austria, the very stronghold of one of the great ecclesiastical systems, a number of these same Bible Students were killed and others imprisoned during the period of the war. In Canada many were haled into court and summarily tried without being given an opportunity to offer a defense, and were fined or imprisoned, the charge being that they had in their possession Bibles with certain comments, hymnbooks which they had used for years in the worship of God, and other literature in harmony with the Scriptures. To the astonishment of many people in the United States there was a wide persecution of conscientious followers of the Master in this land. No Christian permits himself to become embittered because of this unjust treatment, but he recognizes it as a fulfillment of the divine prophecy and one of the evidences given by the Lord to those who yield submissively to the divine arrangement, to assure them that they belong to him. The inspired Apostle wrote: "Beloved, think it not strange concerning the fiery trial which is to try you, as though some strange thing happened unto you: but rejoice, inasmuch as ye are partakers of Christ's suffering; that, when his glory shall be revealed, ye may be glad also with exceeding joy. If ye be reproached for the name of Christ, happy are ye; for the spirit of glory and of God resteth upon you: on their part he is evil spoken of, but on your part he is glorified."-l Peter 4:12-14.

Jesus and the members of his body thus developed through trial and tribulation according to the divine arrangement will constitute the seed of Abraham, through which seed God will ultimately extend blessings to all the families of the earth. The Apostle Paul with prophetic vision looking down through the corridors of the age, marking the suffering of mankind and the development of the Christ class, the seed, exclaimed: "The whole creation groaneth and travaileth in pain together until now, waiting for the manifestation of the Sons of God". -Romans 8:19,22.

Kingdom Coming In

The wars, famine, pestilence, distress of nations, etc., upon the earth are but the forerunners of the establishment of the Messianic kingdom. The Lord through his prophet said: "I will shake all nations, and the desire of all nations shall come." (Haggai 2:7) And while this great shaking is in progress and monarchs are losing their crowns, aristocratic and autocratic thrones are tumbling to the earth, the words of the prophet ring out clearly in the ears of the followers of Jesus: "And in the days of these kings shall the God of heaven set up a kingdom, which shall never be destroyed: and the kingdom shall not be left to other people, but it shall break in pieces and consume all these kingdoms, and it shall stand for ever". -Daniel 2:44.

Elijah was a type of the followers of Christ Jesus; and the Lord used him to picture the events transpiring in the end of the world, as we have heretofore mentioned. (See Pages 19-22) In fulfillment of the antitype, the Elijah class knew that the war was coming and one of them the Lord's faithful servant, Pastor Russell, for forty years pointed out from the prophecies that it would come in 1914. The Lord is not in the war, meaning that the Lord's kingdom is not yet in hill sway. Then follows the earthquake, symbolic of revolution, which has already swept some of the countries. Then shall follow the anarchy-destructive troubles. Anarchy means a disregard of all law, certain classes assuming to exercise power and authority where it is not granted, causing indescribable suffering and sorrow. In this the Lord is not, but it is another means of clearing away the ground preparatory to establishing the kingdom. Then Elijah heard the still small voice. This still small voice is a message from the Lord. The voice is used to symbolize a message or messenger. The Lord has long ago put the message in his Word the Bible for the benefit of those who should live in this hour of stress. The multitudes of earth are clamoring everywhere. They are confused; they are distressed. They are in sorrow, in tears of bitterness. They are almost at their wits' end. But if they could be heard to express their hearts' sincere desire now, without a doubt there would come up from every quarter of the earth this request: Give us a government of righteousness with a wise ruler who will administer the laws in behalf of all; give us peace and not war; give us plenty and not profiteers; give us liberty and not license; give us life and not suffering and death. Back from the past comes the sweet small voice of the Lord saying that this request shall be fulfilled: "For unto us a child is born, unto us a son is given: and the government shall be upon his shoulder: and his name shall be called Wonderful, Counsellor, The mighty God, The everlasting Father, The Prince of Peace. Of the increase of his government and peace there shall be no end, upon the throne of David, and upon his kingdom. to order it, and to establish it with judgment and with justice from henceforth even for ever. The zeal of the Lord of hosts will perform this. - Isaiah 9:6,7.

The Jubilee

An understanding of the jubilee system which Jehovah inaugurated with Israel throws a great light upon the immediate future events. The Scriptures clearly show that Israel, while God dealt with them for more than eighteen centuries, was a typical people. Their law was typical, foreshadowing greater and better things to come. The Lord commanded Moses to institute the Sabbath system the year that Israel entered the land of Canaan, which was 1575 years before A. D. 1 (Leviticus 25:1-12), and that every fiftieth year should be unto them a year of jubilee. This was done on the tenth day of the seventh month, the day of atonement. "And ye shall hallow the fiftieth year and proclaim freedom throughout the land unto all the inhabitants thereof; it shall be a jubilee unto you and ye shall return every man unto his possessions and ye shall return every man unto his family. Other Scriptures show that there were to be seventy jubilees kept. (Jeremiah 25:11; 2 Chronicles 36:17-21) A simple calculation of these jubilees brings us to this important fact: Seventy jubilees of fifty years each would be a total of 3500 years. That period of time beginning 1575 before A. D. 1 of necessity would end in the fall of the year 1925, at which time the type ends and the great antitype must begin. What, then, should we expect to take place? In the type there must be a full restoration; therefore the great antitype must mark the beginning of restoration of all things. The chief thing to be restored is the human race to life; and since other Scriptures definitely fix the fact that there will be a resurrection of Abraham, Isaac, Jacob and other faithful ones of old, and that these will have the first favor, we may expect 1925 to witness the return of these faithful men of Israel from the condition of death, being resurrected and fully restored to perfect humanity and made the visible, legal representatives of the new order of things on earth.

Messiah's kingdom once established, Jesus and his glorified church constituting the great Messiah, shall minister the blessings to the people they have so long desired and hoped for and prayed might come. And when that time comes, there will be peace and not war, as the prophet beautifully states: "In the last days it shall come to pass, that the mountain of the house of the Lord shall be established in the top of the mountains, and it shall be exalted above the hills; and people shall flow unto it. And many nations shall come, and say, Come, and let us go up to the mountain of the Lord, and to the house of the God of Jacob; and he will teach us of his ways, and we will walk in his paths: for the law shall go forth of Zion, and the word of the Lord from Jerusalem. And he shall judge among many people, and rebuke strong nations afar off; and they shall beat their swords into plowshares, and their spears into pruninghooks; nation shall not lift up a sword against nation, neither shall they learn war any more. But they shall sit every man under his vine and under his fig tree; and none shall make them afraid; for the mouth of the Lord of hosts hath spoken it." -Micah 4:1-4.

Earthly Rulers

As we have heretofore stated, the great jubilee cycle is due to begin in 1925. At that time the earthly phase of the kingdom shall be recognized. The Apostle Paul in the eleventh chapter of Hebrews names a long list of faithful men who died before the crucifixion of the Lord and before the beginning of the selection of the church. These can never be a part of the heavenly class; they had no heavenly hopes; but God has in store something good for them. They are to be resurrected as perfect men and constitute the princes or rulers in the earth, according to his promise. (Psalm 45:16; Isaiah 32:1; Matthew 8:11) Therefore we may confidently expect that 1925 will mark the return of Abraham, Isaac, Jacob and the faithful prophets of old, particularly those named by the Apostle in Hebrews chapter eleven, to the condition of human perfection.

Reconstruction

All the statesmen of the world, all the political economists, all the thoughtful men and women, recognize the fact that the conditions existing prior to the war have passed away and that a new order of things must be put in vogue. All such recognize that this is a period now marking the beginning of reconstruction. The great difficulty is that these men are exercising only human wisdom and have ignored the divine arrangement. We are indeed at the time of reconstruction, the reconstruction not only of a few things, but of all things. The reconstruction will not consist of patching up old and broken down systems and forms and arrangements, but the establishment of a new and righteous one under the great ruler Christ Jesus, the Prince of Peace. The Apostle Peter at Pentecost, speaking under divine inspiration, and referring to that time, said: "Times of refreshing shall come from the presence of the Lord; and he shall send Jesus Christ, which before was preached unto you: whom the heaven must receive [retain] until the times of restitution of all things, which God hath spoken by the mouth of all his holy prophets since the world began". - Acts 3:19-21.

Examination of the prophecies from Moses to John discloses the fact that every one of the prophets foretold the time coming for restitution blessings. Reconstruction and restitution mean the same thing-i.e., the restoration of mankind to the things which were lost. The reward of the church in heaven is not that which man originally had; but is given as a great reward for faithfulness to the Lord under trying conditions and circumstances.

Restitution means the blessings that will be given to mankind in general through the divine arrangement and therefore restoring him to life, liberty and happiness on the earth, once enjoyed by the perfect man Adam and which was included in the promise made to Abraham. This blessing comes to the world through the seed, the exalted, elect class, the Messiah, the Christ.
The Scriptures clearly show that this great time of blessing is immediately preceded by a great time of trouble. This trouble is now on the world. The word Michael used in the following text means "who as God", or representing God-Christ Jesus, the great captain of our salvation. His second coming and the establishment of his kingdom has been the hope and desire of Christians for centuries past. In referring to this time, then, the

prophet Daniel under inspiration wrote: "And at that time shall Michael stand up, the great prince which standeth for the children of thy people: and there shall be a time of trouble, such as never was since there was a nation even to that same time: and at that time thy people shall be delivered, every one that shall be found written in the book. And many of them that sleep in the dust of the earth shall awake, some to everlasting life, and some to shame and everlasting contempt."-Daniel 12:1,2.

Millions Will Never Die

Every part of the divine arrangement must be fulfilled; not one jot or tittle shall pass away unfulfilled. Every portion of the divine promise, therefore, is important. Answering the question as to the conditions prevailing at the end of the world, Jesus quoted the above prophetic statement from the Book of Daniel, or used words similar, saying: "Then shall be great tribulation, such as was not since the beginning of the world to this time, no, nor ever shall be. And except those days should be shortened, there should no flesh be saved: but for the elect's sake those days shall be shortened." (Matthew 24:21, 22) Thus he shows that the distress upon the earth will end with a time of tribulation such as the world has never known and that this will be the last. There will never be another. Then he adds that for the sake of the elect those days shall be shortened; and much flesh shall be saved.

We ask, Why would the Lord carry through this time of trouble a large number of people, sparing them from death in the time of trouble, unless he intended to minister unto them some particular blessing? And since God has promised a blessing of restitution to that which Adam lost, and since these promises point to a beginning of fulfillment immediately following this trouble, and since the promise clearly is that the elect, constituting the seed of Abraham, according to the promise. shall be the instruments through which the blessings shall flow, then this statement of Jesus clearly and conclusively proves that many peoples living on earth at the end of the trouble will be the first ones to be offered the blessings of restoration, which blessings will be offered through the elect, the Messiah. It follows as a matter of course that those accepting the offer as made and rendering themselves in obedience to it shall be restored to that which was lost in Adam, viz., life, liberty and happiness.

The prophet of God offers other testimony in corroboration of this: "And it shall come to pass, that in all the land, saith the Lord, two parts therein shall be cut off and die; but the third shall be left therein. And I will bring the third part through the fire, and will refine them as silver is refined, and will try them as gold is tried: they shall call on my name, and I will hear them: I will say, It is my people: and they shall say, The Lord is my God." (Zechariah 13:8, 9) Here, then, is a clear statement to the effect that one part God will spare in this time of trouble and that these shall ultimately be his people and he will be their God.

Having in mind that it was an earthly borne, human life and attendant blessings, that Adam lost, and that these are the blessings God promises shall be restored to man, we can understand the words of the prophet David when he wrote: "Blessed is he that considereth the poor: the Lord will deliver him in time of trouble. The Lord will preserve him, and keep him alive; and he shall be blessed upon the earth; and thou wilt not deliver him unto the will of his enemies." (Psalm 41:1, 2) Here he plainly states that those who deal righteously in this time of trouble shall be blessed upon the earth.

How to Live Forever

The church systems would have the people believe that only those who become church members can be saved. The Bible never taught any such doctrine. The Lord never organized the nominal systems, and the true church is but a little flock, who shall inherit the kingdom of heaven, and the others of the world to not inherit it. To the church Jesus said: "Fear not, little flock; for it is your Father's good pleasure to give you the kingdom". (Luke 12:32) Jesus died not only for those who will constitute the members of the church, but for all. St. John plainly stated: "He is the propitiation [satisfaction] for our sins: and not for ours only, but also for the sins of the whole world".-l John 2:2. The Apostle Paul, discussing the great Redeemer and his office, said: "We see Jesus, who was made a little lower than the angels for the suffering of death, crowned with glory and honor; that he by the grace of God should taste death for every man. For it became him, for whom are all things, and by whom are all things, in bringing many Sons unto glory, to make the captain of their salvation perfect through sufferings." (Hebrews 2:9, 10) Thus we see that Jesus died for every man, not only for a few. Again says the Apostle: "There is one God, and one mediator between God and men, the man Christ Jesus; who gave himself a ransom for all, to be testified in due time". (1 Timothy 2:5, 6) By this Scripture it is clearly seen that in God's due time every creature must hear the testimony as to what Jesus has done for him and know of the plan of salvation. Again says the Apostle Paul: "The gift of God is eternal life through Jesus Christ our Lord". (Romans 6:23) There can be no gift without both a giver and a receiver, and this could not operate without knowledge on the part of both. In other words, the giver must intelligently offer the gift to another, and the other must intelligently know of this fact before he can receive it. It would be impossible for the human race, therefore, to accept the gift of life everlasting before it is offered. It will be offered only in God's due time and the divine plan shows that his due time is after the seed of promise is developed, after the kingdom is set up; and then each one in his order will be brought to a knowledge of the fact that a plan of redemption exists and that the way is open for him to accept the terms of it and live. Knowledge being essential, it precedes the reception of blessings from the Lord; and knowing this fact, it is easy to be seen why the adversary, the devil, and his agencies so diligently strive to prevent the people from knowing the truth. But when Messiah's kingdom is established we are definitely informed (Revelation 20:1-4) that Satan will be restrained of his power that he might deceive the nations no more; and then the people shall know the truth and nothing shall hinder them from knowing it.

Positive Promise

The words of Jesus must be given full force and effect because he spake as never man spake. His speech was with absolute authority. And in God's due time his words must have a fulfillment, and they cannot have a fulfillment until that due time. Jesus plainly said: "Verily, verily, I say unto you, If a man keep my saying, he shall never see death". (John 8:51) As above stated, no one could keep the saying of Jesus until he hears it, until he has a knowledge of God's arrangement. Throughout the Gospel age none but Christians have had this knowledge and all who have kept this saying and keep it faithfully until the end will receive life everlasting on the divine plane. (Revelation 2:10) The remainder of mankind have not heard it; therefore could not keep it. They will hear, however, in due time after the establishment of the kingdom. Then it shall come to pass that every one who will keep the saying of the Lord shall never see death. This promise would not have been made by Jesus if he did not intend to carry it into full force and effect in due time.

Again he said: "Whosoever liveth and believeth in me shall never die". (John 11:26) Do we believe the Masters statement? If so, when the time comes for the world to know, then they who believe and, of course, render themselves in obedience to the terms have the absolute and positive statement of Jesus that they shall never die.

Based upon the argument heretofore set forth, then, that the old order of things, the old world, is ending and is therefore passing away, and that the new order is coming in, and that 1925 shall mark the resurrection of the faithful worthies of old and the beginning of reconstruction, it is reasonable to conclude that millions of people now on the earth will be still on the earth in 1925. Then, based upon the promises set forth in the divine Word, we must reach the positive and indisputable conclusion that millions now living will never die.

Of course, it does not mean that every one will live; for some will refuse to obey the divine law; but those who have been evil and turn again to righteousness and obey righteousness shall live and not die. Of this we have the positive statement of the Lord's prophet, as follows:

"When the wicked man turneth away from his wickedness that he hath committed, and doeth that which is lawful and right, he shall save his soul alive. Because he considereth, and turneth away from all his transgressions that he hath committed, he shall surely live, he shall not die." - Ezekiel 18:27, 28.

Returning Youth

The Lord, in the exercise of his loving-kindness toward man, has graciously given many illustrations and pictures of the outworkings of his great plan. In the book of Job he gives us a picture of the perfection of man, of his fall, of the redemption by the great Ransomer, and then the subsequent restoration. When the times of restoration begin there will doubtless be many men on the earth who will be very old and almost ready for the tomb. But those who learn of the great ransom-sacrifice and who accept the Ransomer shall return to the days of their youth; they shall be restored to perfection of body and mind and live on the earth forever. We note the words of the prophet:

"He [Jehovah] keepeth back his [man's] soul from the pit, and his life from perishing by the sword. He [man] is chastened also with pain upon his bed, and the multitude of his bones with strong pain: so that his life abhorreth bread, and his soul dainty meat. His flesh is consumed away, that it cannot be seen; and his bones that were not seen stick out. Yea, his soul draweth near unto the grave, and his life to the destroyers."

Thus is given a vivid description of the dying human race, individually and collectively. Then the prophet shows how the message of truth will be brought to him and he will learn of the great ransom-sacrifice. Continuing, he says: "If there be a messenger [one who brings a message of glad tidings] with him [man], an interpreter [one who expounds and makes it clear], one among a thousand [the Lord will provide here and there teachers for the benefit of others], to show unto man his [the Lord's] uprightness: then be [the Lord] is gracious unto him [man], and saith, Deliver him from going down to the pit [grave: and the man joyfully says:] I have found a ransom. His flesh shall be fresher than a child's: he shall return to the days of his youth."-Job 33:18-25.

When God expelled Adam from Eden he said: "And now, lest he [Adam] put forth his hand, and take also of the tree of life, and eat, and live for ever: therefore the Lord God sent him forth from the garden of Eden, . . . and he placed at the east of the garden of Eden cherubims, and a flaming sword which turned every way, to keep the way of the tree of life". (Genesis 3:22-24) Thus the Word shows that had Adam remained in Eden, feeding upon the perfect food it afforded, he would have continued to live. The judgment was executed against him by causing him to feed upon imperfect food. Perfect food, therefore, seems a necessary element to sustain human life everlastingly. When the kingdom of Messiah is inaugurated, the great Messiah will make provision for right food conditions.

Thus, when restoration begins, a man of seventy years of age will gradually be restored to a condition of physical health and mental balance. The Lord will teach him how to eat, what to eat, and other habits of life; and above all, the truth, and how to think and how to fix his mind upon holy things. And by the gradual process of restoration he will be lifted up by the great Mediator and restored to the days of his youth and live on the earth forever and never see death.

Resurrection

Not only will those living on the earth when restoration begins have the opportunity of life, but all the dead shall be awakened and brought back in their regular order and likewise be given an opportunity for life. It was the great Master who declared: "Marvel not at this: for the hour is coming, in the which all that are in the graves shall hear his voice, and shall come forth". (John 5:28, 29) St. Paul plainly says: "There shall be a resurrection of the dead, both of the just and unjust". (Acts 24:15) In his clear, forceful and logical argument set out in 1 Corinthians 15, St. Paul conclusively proves that the resurrection of Jesus Christ is a guarantee that every one of the dead shall be awakened and brought to a knowledge of the truth. Then he says: "He [God] hath appointed a day, in the which he will judge the world in righteousness by that man whom he hath ordained; whereof he hath given assurance unto all men, in that he hath raised him from the dead" (Acts 17:31); thus showing that during the reign of the Messiah every one shall have one fair and impartial opportunity for the blessings of life, liberty and happiness.

The brave young men who went to war and died upon the battlefield have not gone to heaven, nor to eternal torture, as the creeds of Christendom would make their loved ones believe. They have not shed their bodies and gone floating about in space, as the spiritists would make men believe. They are dead, waiting for the resurrection; and in due time they shall be brought back to the condition of life and restored to their loved ones and be given a full opportunity to accept the terms of the new order of things and live forever. Many a good mother has spent sleepless nights and wept tears of bitterness because of her loved one that died upon the battlefield. Many a sweetheart, many a father, many a child, has likewise been bowed down in sorrow because of the great suffering that the war, trouble and death entailed upon the people.

Clergy's Opportunity

What a wonderful opportunity the clergy have had and neglected during the past five years of distress! Instead of misleading the people into erroneous ways, where they have found sorrow reigning in the home because of the death of loved ones, because of the loss upon the battlefield of some dear one, what a splendid opportunity to call attention to the precious promises of the Scriptures! For instance, to say to the weeping mother: "Thus saith the Lord: ...Refrain they voice from weeping, and thine eyes from tears; for thy work shall be rewarded, saith the Lord; and they shall come again from the land of the enemy. And there is hope in thine end, saith the Lord, that thy children shall come again to their own border." (Jeremiah 31:15-17) The land of the enemy is the land of death, because death is the great enemy; and the Lord will call back all who have gone into that condition, and during his reign he will destroy death.-1 Corinthians 15:25, 26.

Appeal to the Clergy

It is not my thought to hold up the clergy to ridicule, but rather would I appeal to them that they fulfil their duty and obligation to the people in this hour of distress. I would remind them that the commission given to all followers of Jesus is not to convert the world and bring them into some organized system. Their commission is not to collect money from the people to carry out these purposes. Their commission is not to persecute others. But their divinely given commission is plainly set forth by the Lord in these words: "The Spirit of the Lord God is upon me; because the

Lord hath anointed me to preach good tidings unto the meek; he hath sent me to bind up the brokenhearted, to proclaim liberty to the captives, and the opening of the prison to them that are bound; to proclaim the acceptable year of the Lord, and the day of vengeance of our God; to comfort all that mourn; to appoint unto them that mourn in Zion, to give unto them beauty for ashes, the oil of joy for mourning, the garment of praise for the spirit of heaviness; that they might be called trees of righteousness, the planting of the Lord, that he might be glorified." - Isaiah 61:1-3.

Never was there such a time to bind up the brokenhearted; never such a time to comfort those that mourn, as now. Why not tell the people the beautiful, wonderful truths contained in the Bible and thereby enable them to look beyond the distress that afflicts mankind, to the new day that is coming in when life, liberty, happiness and blessings will be offered to all mankind!

Great Joy Coming

It was life, liberty and happiness that Adam possessed and lost. These things Jesus purchased by his own blood. In the time of his reign he will give liberty to all the prisoners in the prison-house of death and under the domination of the adversary, as beautifully declared by the prophet, thus establishing full liberty in the earth: "Behold my servant, whom I uphold; mine elect, in whom my soul delighteth; I have put my spirit upon him: he shall bring forth judgment to the Gentiles. He shall not cry, nor lift up, nor cause his voice to be heard in the street. A bruised reed shall he not break, and the smoking flax shall he not quench: he shall bring forth judgment unto truth. He shall not fail nor be discouraged, till he have set judgment in the earth: and the isles shall wait for his law. Thus saith God the Lord, he that created the heavens, and stretched them out; he that spread forth the earth, and that which cometh out of it; he that giveth bread unto the people upon it, and spirit to them that walk therein: I the Lord have called thee in righteousness, and will hold thine band, and will keep thee, and give thee for a covenant of the people, for a light of the Gentiles; to open the blind eyes, to bring out the prisoners from the prison, and them that alt in darkness out of the prison-house."-Isaiah 42:1-7.

We have heretofore set forth how the Lord will minister life everlasting to all the obedient ones under his glorious reign. And when these favors are returned it will indeed be a time of happiness-a happiness that will come to stay. God's prophet, looking down to that time, under inspiration of the Holy Spirit, wrote: "The ransomed of the Lord [the whole human race] shall return [from the condition of bondage to sin and death], and come to Zion [the Messiah] with songs and everlasting joy upon their heads: they shall obtain joy and gladness, and sorrow and sighing shall flee away". -Isaiah 35:10. Then the prophet in beautiful phrase pictures how the earth itself shall become a fit habitation for man. The wilderness and the solitary place will blossom as the rose, and streams shall break forth in the desert; the earth will yield its increase, and everything in the earth give praise to God for the fulfillment of his wonderful promises.

This is the Golden Age of which the prophets prophesied and of which the Psalmist sang; and it is the privilege of the student of the divine Word today, by the eye of faith. to see that we are standing at the very portals of that blessed time! Let us look up and lift up our heads. Deliverance is at the door!

Glorious Climax

The Messiah, the Christ in glory, will constitute the new invisible ruling power; therefore designated in the Scriptures as the new heaven. The righteous government organized in the earth will constitute what the Scriptures symbolically speak of as the new earth - the earthly phase of the Lord's kingdom. St. Peter stated that the faithful ones, according to God's promise, look for such "new heavens and a new earth, wherein dwelleth righteousness" -2 Peter 3:13.

When John the Revelator was serving his sentence on the isle of Patmos, our Lord showed approval of him and visited him and graciously granted to him a marvelous vision, which is recorded as a part of the Holy Scriptures. With ecstasy that inspired witness of the Lord wrote: "And I saw a new heaven [invisible ruling power] and a new earth [organized society]: for the first heaven and the first earth [the old order] were passed away; and there was no more sea. And I John saw the holy City [the kingdom of Messiah], new Jerusalem, coming down from God out of heaven, prepared as a bride adorned for her husband. And I heard a great voice out of heaven saying, Behold, the tabernacle of God is with men, and he will dwell with them, and they shall be his people, and God himself shall be with them, and be their God. And God shall wipe away all tears from their eyes; and there shall be no more death, neither sorrow, nor crying, neither shall there be any more pain: for the former things are passed away. And he that sat upon the throne said, Behold, I make all things new. And he said unto me, Write: for these words are true and faithful." - Revelation 21:1-5.

No one can gainsay this positive and conclusive promise that under the Messiah's reign death shall be destroyed, and sorrow, sighing and crying shall cease, and that all who are obedient shall be restored to life, liberty and happiness. And since the old order is passing away and the new is coming in, we can with confidence proclaim the glad message that millions now living on the earth will be granted the opportunity for life everlasting and those who obey shall never die, but shall be restored and live in happiness, joy and peace upon the earth forever.

Reader, have you found the foregoing Pages of interest? Would you like to have further detailed and corroborative proof establishing beyond a doubt that the war, profiteering, famine, pestilence, the falling away of the clergy and their union with the financial powers and professional politicians to oppress mankind, were long ago foretold in the Bible? If so, at once supply yourself with a copy of "The Finished Mystery".

"The Finished Mystery" is the first and only book that has ever made clear the prophecies of Revelation and Ezekiel. It supplies additional detailed and abundant proof that the present unrighteous systems must be shortly supplanted by Messiah's government of righteousness in the earth, in which every honest man is interested. Your personal interest and that of your family demand that you read "The Finished Mystery".

It is obtainable from the International Bible Students Association, Brooklyn, New York, U.S.A., at the nominal cost of $1.00. See advertisement on Page 126.

Bible Citations in Substantiation

Compiled by C. J. Woodworth

GENESIS

1:26. God designs that man shall have the dominion of earth. He does not have that dominion yet, as explained in Hebrews 2:8,9, and he cannot have it until the Life-Giver returns and gives it.

1:28. If it is God's purpose to fill the earth with a race that shall be all righteous as declared by the prophet, Isaiah 60:21. The basin of the Amazon is so rich that nothing but a population of swarming billions could ever subdue the rank vegetation.

2:2, 3. It was the divine plan that man should have six one-thousand year days of toil under the great taskmaster, Sin, to be followed by a seventh one-thousand-year day of rest from it. This is here foreshadowed.

2:8,9. This is a picture of what the whole world is to become. The work we now see everywhere going on about us, of beautifying the earth, is part of the preparation for Messiah's reign.

3:15. The Messiah is to have the power to destroy Satan and all the works of Satan, one of which is death. When Messiah reigns, Satan will no longer have power to lead men into sin and death.

3:21. This looks forward to the sacrifice of the Lamb of God, and thus to provision for redeeming man from the curse of death.

3:22-24. God purposes that man shall live forever upon earth.

4:4. Abel's sacrifice looked forward to the all-sufficient one.

4:8. Abel's death represented the death of the Christ; it is the death of these that makes the future blessings sure.

8:21. In the passing over from "this present evil world" to "the world to come" God will not smite all, but will save some alive.

9:11. All flesh shall not be cut off again.

9:15. Again, "Millions now living will never die".

12:3. When the due time comes for blessing all the families of the earth, those then living will be due for a blessing also.

13:15, 16. Some are promised an everlasting earthly inheritance.

13:17. Abraham's promised inheritance is to be on the earth.

15:7-21. The word here rendered "whereby" conveys the thought of, "Please give me all the information available on the subject." The Lord answered in signs which we summarize:

Eleven symbolic years, the combined ages of these animals, equal 3,960 literal years. They begin to count, as appears from Genesis 16:3, "after

Abram had dwelt ten years in the land of Canaan" and this, as the Bible chronology shows, was about October 1, 2,036 B.C. 2,0351/4 years brings us down to the A.D. period and 1,9243/4 brings us to the full end of the 3,960. 1,924 full years of the A.D. period will end December 31, 1924 A.D. and 3/4 years more ends about October 1, 1925 A.D., at which time there is reason to believe that Abraham will come into possession of his inheritance.

The attendant phenomena seem to suggest that the vision will be fulfilled during the time of trouble, pictured by the "smoking furnace" at a time when the Lord Jesus will be present in his second advent as the light of the world, pictured as a "burning lamp". As ten is a symbol of national completeness the ten nations here mentioned seem to represent all the nations of the earth.

17:8. The everlasting inheritance of Abraham and his posterity is to be on earth. As some will never die and the time for them to appear is near it is reasonable to infer that co-inheritors now will never die, and there are millions of them.

17: 17-19. The name of Isaac, meaning "laughter"; the fact that he typified the Christ, as explained in Galatians 4:28; and the fact that he was the blesser of all his brethren, as here prophesied, prove that there will come a time when millions will never die.

18:18. All the nations of the earth, including the dead nations are here promised a blessing, implying their resurrection. When that time comes the living will be blessed with opportunities for life also.

19:17-22. As Lot and his two daughters were delivered from the destruction of literal Sodom and given a little city to live in, so it may be that many will be delivered from the destruction of churchianity, "that city which is spiritually called Sodom", Revelation 11:8, and permitted to live on into the new order of things.

21:14-19. The hopes of the world are knit up with the hopes of fleshly Israel, whom Ishmael represented, even as Isaac represented spiritual Israel. The hopes of Zionists were revived at the great Hippodrome meeting in 1910 when Pastor Russell delivered his address on Zionism in Prophecy to 5,500 Jews. Here the antitipical Ishmael, ready to die of thirst, was supplied with just the water of life most needed. This is a sign of the early approach of returning favor to the Jew, new manifest in Zionism.

22:7, 8, 13. The lamb caught in the thicket represented Jesus, the blesser of all the living and the dead.

22:18. The living nations will participate in these blessings.

25:1-4. Keturah represented the New Covenant, God's means for fulfilling the Abrahamic Covenant and blessing all mankind. She had six sons, representing that her offspring, at first, are imperfect. But she had ten grandsons, symbol of national completeness, symbolizing that, in the end, the whole world will own The New Covenant as their source of life, and by it will reach perfection.

26:3. The living nations will participate in these blessings.

28:12. A vision of our Lord Jesus in his capacity as the Savior of mankind bringing blessings of life to all, living and dead.

28:14. The living families will participate in these blessings. 35:18. The fact that we now see the time of nominal Zion's travail argues that the time for the blessing of mankind is near. Benjamin, in a way, brought blessings to his other brethren.

45:3-5. This revelation of Joseph to his brethren prior to his blessing of them represents the second advent of our Lord now being gradually revealed to the world to their ultimate joy.

49:10. Shiloh is Christ, the Prince of Peace, the peacemaker between heaven and earth. When he begins to draw all men unto himself it will include the millions now living as well as the dead.

50:17. This represents the spirit of prayer and supplication as it will shortly be poured out upon millions now living.

50:20. As God was pleased to save much people alive at the hands of Joseph, so there is reason to believe he will be equally pleased to save alive millions now living at the hands of Christ.

EXODUS

3:8. This represents the purpose of the second advent of Christ.

4:4. This represents God's purpose to lay hold upon present evil conditions, banishing sin and death and every evil thing.

5:17. This sign preceding Israel's deliverance from Egypt we now see preceding mankind's deliverance from Satan's empire.

7:12. This sign preceding Israel's deliverance shows how our clear comprehension of the reason for the permission of evil completely obliterates by its greater power previous explanations. 7:20. This sign shows how the millions of tracts setting forth the blessed harvest tidings would seem to churchianity. This sign, fulfilled, shows that the time for earths deliverance is near.

The succeeding chapters of Exodus, down to 12:30 inclusive, narrating the plagues successively of frogs, lice, flies, murrain, boils, hail, locusts, darkness and the death of the firstborn. represent successive manifestations of God's power in setting forth the truth. Among the antitypes of these plagues we see the seven volumes of Studies in the Scriptures. The fact that these have all been published shows that the deliverance of the world is nigh.

14:29, 30. The passage of Israel through the Red Sea may represent that some will pass through the time of anarchy alive.

15:13. This applies to the whole world of mankind.

15:26. This promise to fleshly Israel applies also to the world of mankind to the end of the gospel age.

16:21. As the Israelites gathered the manna fresh every morning so the world in the new age will need to seek supplies of grace to live. This will apply to those living when the day of grace dawns.

16:23. It was the divine plan that man should have a great Sabbath day for recovery of living and dead from sin and death.

19:10, 11. This third day represents the early morning of the third thousand-year day beginning with the thousand-year day in which the ransom was provided for the living as well as the dead.

20:8-10. The Sabbath day typified the great thousand-year Sabbath day of restitution for the living as well as the dead.

28:33. The bells of gold represent that when the King shall come the fruits of his redemptive work will be manifest to all.

32:34. This leading of the people into the promised land represents the leading back of all who will into harmony with God.

34:30. The bright-shining of which Israel was afraid represents the time of trouble which the world will not be able to endure. Following this the greater than Moses, Christ, will speak to the living and the dead through the medium of the veil, the Ancient Worthies.

LEVITICUS

9:23. This appearance of the glory of the Lord unto all the people represented the time soon coming when "the glory of the Lord [his love for all men, living and dead] shall be revealed" to all.

13:2. This represents the arrangement of the Lord for the healing of all mankind, living and dead, from sin, in the new age.

14:4. The cedar wood represents the everlasting life that may be obtained by living and dead in the Millennial age, the scarlet the blood of the ransom, the hyssop the cleansing Word.

14:12. The trespass offerings represent the means of reconciliation shortly to be opened for the living as well as the dead.

18:5. Those who will keep the new laws may live everlastingly.

23:3. The Sabbath day typified the great thousand-year Sabbath day of recovery of the living and dead from sin and death.

25:10. This represents the coming deliverance of all, living and dead.
26:18,24,28. The seven Gentile times ended in the fall of 1914.

26:34. 35, 40-45. A reference to the seventy jubilees which must pass over Israel before they really enter the promised land. These 3500 years began with the entrance into Canaan in the spring of 1575 B.C., 15743/4 years before the A.D. era end will come to their full end in 19241/4, o about April 1, 1925, at which time we may expect the resurrection of the Ancient Worthies and the beginning of the blessing of all the families of the earth, living as well as dead. The last year of the 3,500 years will be itself a jubilee year witnessing the antitype, the great jubilee, of restitution.

27:24. Another reference to the coming deliverance of all men.

NUMBERS

14:31-34. The last verse of this citation is one of the keys that unlock the time prophecies and one, therefore, by which we discern that the world has ended. There seems to be a parallelism in the preceding verses between the experiences of the professed people of God in this harvest time and the experiences of fleshly Israel there. We may see that the forty years wandering of spiritual Israel began in the fell of 1881. The ten unfaithful spies, the worldly clergy, rejected the restitution message as an awful message, a devilish message, and the people heeded them instead of heeding the truth. but it may well be that, literally, they and their systems shall fall to enter in, while their children, literally, shall have the promised inheritance. It may be that these worldly systems will go down lo the fall of 1921. Or the forty years may be viewed as beginning with the proclamation of the harvest message in 1878 and ending with the beginning of the downfall of ecclesiasticism, which took place in Russia lo 1918.

19:9. These ashes of the red heifer, kept for the cleansing of the people from sin, represent the remembrance of the faithfulness of the Ancient Worthies which will be available for all ere long.

21:9. The serpent of brass represented sin, Satan's agent in luring our first parents into condemnation, hence our Lord Jesus who took the place of the sinner, living and dead.

DEUTERONOMY

4:9-11. These words, applicable to Israel at the inauguration of the old Law Covenant, will be applicable to all mankind, living and dead, at the inauguration of the new Law Covenant. The fulfillment of these symbols we now see going on about us.

4:40. Under the new Law Covenant Israel and, by extension, old mankind, living and dead, may, if obedient, live forever.

5:12-14. Fleshly Israel's day of rest typified the coming time in which the whole, world, living and dead, shall rest from sin.

5:16. Those may live forever who honor Jehovah and the New Covenant, represented here by father and mother.

18:15-18. A prophecy of the coming offer of life to all.

28:1-14. Representing the blessings coming upon all the world, living and dead, with the advent of the new Law Covenant.

30:15, 19. These words apply to all the world, living and dead, in the dawn of the new age. They have never yet had fulfillment; never yet has a real offer of life for the living been held out to any.

32:43. This rejoicing of the nations of earth with Israel has not yet taken place, but it will take place for both living and dead.

JOSHUA

1:11. The three days' preparation of victuals represent the thousand-year day in which Christ was crucified and the two succeeding ones in which the church is gathered out. Upon this food the world, living and dead, will feed in the age almost at hand.

5:12. Representing new offers of life to millions living.

6:20. This represents the utter overthrow of the powers of sin, and the end of all necessity for any man to die. Already we see the walls of the antitypical Jericho, churchianity, tottering.

14:10. This keeping of Caleb alive from the time Israel left Egypt until the promised land had been conquered and divided represents how some will go over into the new age without dying.

JUDGES

3:9. The judges of ancient times were not only rulers but deliverers. The present commotion in the earth is due to the fact that the Judge is here and the judgment day is under way. The Judge not only will suppress all wrong but will hold out life for all.

1. SAMUEL

2:6. Soon none will need longer to go into the grave.

11:12, 13. In some senses of the word the first king of Israel represented earth's new king- "not willing that any should perish".

2. SAMUEL

7:10. When the time has come that Israel shall "dwell in a place of their own and move no more" the time will also have come when "millions now living will never die".

19:21, 22. David was a type of earth's coming king-"not willing that any should perish".

1. KINGS

1:51, 52. Solomon similarly was a type of earth's coming king.

8:56. The rest from their enemies which came upon fleshly Israel represents the real rest coming upon all the living and dead.

2. KINGS

4:5, 6. This pouring out of the oil represents the pouring out of the holy spirit upon all flesh, living and dead. Every vessel fitted for its reception shall be filled to the full with Gods spirit.

1. CHRONICLES

16:31-34. The judgment day, which we have already entered, is a time of hope and blessing for all mankind, living and dead.

17:9. A permanent dwelling place signifies the end of death.

2. CHRONICLES

36:21. A reference to the seventy jubilees beginning in the spring of 1575 B.C. and ending in the spring of 1925. When these jubilees are complete the time will have come for blessing all.

NEHEMIAH

8:5-12. This reading of the law by Ezra and the aid rendered by his thirteen assistants, followed by the rejoicing of the people, seems to represent the coming unfolding of his Word by the lord, the cooperation of the twelve tribes of spiritual Israel and the great company, and the subsequent joy of all, living and dead.

JOB

33:14-30. Elihu, not one of the three contenders with Job that were reproved by the Almighty, but a fourth one whose utterances seem to have been guided by the Lord, calls attention to the fact that God has repeatedly warned mankind during this night time of evil: that man has seen strange visions upon his creed bed throughout this period, but now that we are in the day of wrath he is getting his eyes and ears open. No longer shall man be permitted to follow their own plans. Then follows the history of a man that is sick, his pains, his failing appetite, his loss of flesh, all suggesting his speedy dissolution. Then he explains that if the time has come for the second advent of the Lord, the Messenger of the Covenant, God's interpreter of his own character, the fairest among ten thousand, God is gracious unto the sick one and says, in substance, He need not die, the ransom has been applied for him; if he will repent of his sins he may grow young again and live forever." 38 11-15. Evil is permitted only to a certain extent. Here its coming end is shown as associated with the fixed time for the coming of the Dayspring from on high. When he comes, in the language of verse 14 (Leeser) "She is changed as the sealing clay and all things stand as though newly clad". All things shall be made new; death shall be no more.

42:12. Job's experiences picture the experiences of those of mankind that shall live through the time of anarchy.

PSALMS

2:1-12. This entire psalm has particular reference to our day.

4:3. The kind of people that will be spared in the day of wrath.

5:37. Hare is a prayer that the world of mankind may well pray in their morning, a prayer that they may not be destroyed.

5:11,12. Those whom the Lord defends and blesses in the time of trouble need not pass into death.

6:4, 5, 9. David's prayer to be delivered out of death, and its favorable answer afford encouragement to millions now living.

7:9, 10. In the Millennial age the wickedness of the wicked will come to an end and the just shall be established, defended, saved.

8:1-9. God's original purpose to have man as the lord of his earthly dominion is here stated, and there is also a reference to the divine determination to visit him, which will mean his life spared.

9:9, 10. This promise would seem to be particularly appropriate to those living in the greatest of all times of trouble.

10:16. When the heathen are perished out of the earth there will be no occasion for anybody else to perish, but all may live.

11:6, 7. When the wicked are destroyed others will be preserved.

13:3-6. A prayer especially appropriate to those now living.

15:1-5. After the time of trouble there will be only one mountain or hill left, the kingdom of God, represented by Mount Moriah. This Psalm shows who alone may dwell permanently in it.

16:11. The parable of the sheep and the goats, Matthew 25: 31-46 shows that those on the right hand of earth's new king need never die, even as here suggested.

17:4. Words peculiarly appropriate for some of the world at this time.

18:12-14. These signs that the world has ended are here.

22:27-28. When all the kindreds of the nations worship before the Lord none will need to die. The Lord, as governor, is at the door.

24:3-5. Shows who may permanently dwell in the kingdom.

25:12, 13. A promise for millions now living that will never die.

27: 1-14. This entire Psalm seems to be one in which the poor world can take special comfort in this evil day.

30: 1-12. This Psalm of rejoicing will be appropriate to the millions now living that are carried through the time of trouble.

31:22-24. Words appropriate for those who are spared.

32:6-11. Other words appropriate to the world now.

33:18-22. A promise that millions now living will never die.

34:11-22. Words addressed to millions now living.

35:9, 10. With the close of the time of trouble the Lord will deliver man from the power of "him that is too strong for him".

36:7-10. Words appropriate for millions now living.

37:1-40. This entire Psalm is filled with direct evidence that there are millions now living that will never die.

41:1-3. A promise that millions now living will never die.

45:16, 17. There are to be princes in all the earth and a people there that shall praise the Lord for ever and ever without death.

46:1-11. This Psalm shows that the world has ended.

47:7, 8. When God is king over all the earth, reigning over the (now) heathen nations, there will be blessings of life for all.

49:7. But God provided one who could give a ransom price.

53:6. This rejoicing will be on the part of the living.

55:22, 23. The destruction of the bloody and deceitful, coupled with the statement that the righteous shall not be moved, is evidence that there will be a time when some will not need do die.

59:16. God's mercy and power to deliver from the grave are do be made manifest in the Millennial morning.

60:2-4. Evidences that the world has ended.

65:5. God is not yet the confidence of the ends of all the earth but when he is, death will be no more.

66:4. When all the earth worships God death will be at an end.

67:1-7. God's saving health is to be made known among all nations. This whole Psalm is appropriate to this, our day.

68:1-3. The destruction of the wicked implies that the righteous will not be destroyed; indeed, the text says they shall be glad.

69:35, 36. This language seems to imply that certain Jews will have a permanent inheritance in the land, and that inheritance will be shared by others, including some now living.

72:2-7. The breaking in pieces of Satan, the great oppressor, implies that his reign of death shall end. The condition of man now is like that of mown grass. He is on the way to death, but the return of Christ will bring life as showers to dying grass.

72:12-14. The poor world needs life and redemption from the violence of death and their cry shall be heard.

72:16. Here is promised prolonged life for those who dwell in the cities, now admittedly the hardest places to sustain life.

76:8, 9. Now, in the judgment day, God will save the meek.

82:1-5. Evidence that the world has ended.

84:11. Now that the due time has come God will not withhold the gift of continued life from those that walk uprightly.

86:9. When the due time comes for the dead nations to come forth and worship God millions then living will never die.

89:15. The joyful sound is that the King has come, bringing life not only to the dead but to the living.

90:3. Shortly none will need to continue going into destruction.

92:9-12. When the enemies of the Lord perish those who are not his enemies may continue to live, to flourish like the palm tree.

94:20-23. When the Lord cuts off the wicked in their iniquity, especially those who frame their mischief into laws for the suppression of his truth, the innocent will be spared from like fate.

96:1, 10-13. The new song is that the King has come to bring life to the dead and the living.

97:1-6. Evidences that the world has ended. When all the people see (understand) the Lord's glory none will longer need to die.

98:2. Here the complete evangelization of the world is shown and when this time arrives none will longer need to die.

100:1-5. When all lands unite in praise of the Lord's mercy death will be at an end.

101:5-8. When the slanderers, the proud, the deceitful and the wicked are cut off, the faithful and perfect of heart may live on.

102:19, 20, 28. Evidence that millions now living will never die.

103:19. When the Lord's kingdom rules over all none need die.

104:5. The earth is designed to be the home of an everlasting race. God did not design to fill the earth with dying creatures.

104:35. When the wicked are no more the righteous may live on. 107:11-16. Our parents in Eden rebelled against God's Word, set at naught his counsel and fell down, in labor, under the curse of death. Out from this curse they are shown here as emerging, the bands which have been hastening them toward the brass gates and iron bars of the tomb having been sundered

107:24-31. Here we have a picture of present conditions indicating that the world has ended, and accompanying it is the statement that the Lord will bring peace and life out of the turmoil.

110:3-6. Here is represented; the submission of earth's peoples to the Lord in the day of his power and such submission will bring life. The last verse supplies evidence that the world has ended.

112:4. The greatest light that can arise upon man in this land of darkness is the Sun of Righteousness, bringing compassion and life.

113:3-8. Here is evidence that the Lord shall be praised everywhere and that in that day some of the poor and needy of mankind will be given life and a place with the Ancient Worthies.

115:16-18. Words appropriate for millions now living.

116:6-9. The Lord will preserve some from going into death.

118:15-23. "I shall not die. but live" is a theme for today.

119:119. The putting away of the wicked implies life to others.

119144. An assurance of continued life to the wise toward God.

125: 4, 5. The crooked and the workers of iniquity are to go into death but good (life) is to be to the upright.

139:24. The righteous may be led in the way everlasting.

140:11-13. The violent will be overthrown along with the evil speakers, but the upright will be privileged to live on.

145:9-2 1. The twentieth verse is direct evidence that those that love the Lord need not die when the wicked are destroyed, and the balance of the context is all appropriate to that thought.

PROVERBS

2:20, 21. Direct evidence that some will continue to live on. 3:1,2. Here some are promised long life and peace and this life and peace may be everlasting.

3:13-18. Length of days and the tree of life promised to some.

11:31. some of the righteous will be rewarded with everlasting human life When that time comes millions now living need not die.

29:2. All will rejoice over Christ's righteous rule and live on.

ECCLESIASTES

1:4. God designed the earth to be the permanent home of man, and although now the generations succeed one another in death yet death shall cease, as other Scriptures show.

CANTICLES

2:8-13, 17. Here is evidence that the world has ended and that the world's springtime of hope and of life has come.

4:6. A reference to the dawn of the day of life for the world.

5:9. Inquiry is the first step to hearing and hearing is the first step toward life. This text is located in the immediate future.

ISAIAH

1:9. Since Brother Russell applies verse 3 to nominal Christendom, this verse may apply to the millions who will not die, but who will be a very small remnant compared to the billions of dead.

1:19. Continued life will be the reward of willingness.

1:24-31. Evidence that the world has ended, the transgressors are to be destroyed and the judges (life-givers) restored.

2:2-4. When the time comes that many nations and peoples desire to join themselves to the Lord death will cease.

2:7, 8. An evidence that the world has ended.

2:11. When Jehovah is exalted in the hearts of men there will be no occasion for death to continue.

2:20. Evidence of the end of the world.

3:5. Evidences that the world has ended. Compare 2 Timothy 3. "In the last days perilous times shall come", etc.

3:10. The righteous shall eat the fruit of their own doings.

3:12. In the end of the age preachers cause the people to err.

4:2-6. Direct evidence that millions now living will never die.

5:7. An evidence of the end of the age.

6:13. An hint that possibly one-tenth will live on forever.

8:21 to 9:7. Evidence that the world has ended and an everlasting era of peace is at hand. In this era death shall cease.

11:4-9. Nothing shall hurt nor destroy. Death will cease.

11:12-16. An evidence that the world has ended.

12:1-6. When the world of mankind is joyfully drawing water out of the wells of salvation they will appreciate this prophecy.

14:7. Rest from every foe, including death, is here promised.

16:5. When lasting righteousness prevails in the earth none will longer need to die.

18:3. The seventh trumpet marks the jubilee of earth, the end of death and of dying.

19:21-25. Here is pictured the healing of the sin-sick world.

21:12. Earth's time of inquiry after God is after her trouble.

24:6. A direct statement that there will be some men left after the time of trouble has swept the earth.

24:16-23. Evidences that the world has ended. The glorious reign of the Prince of Life also made known.

25:6-12. A feast of fat nourishing things provided; death is condemned to be swallowed up in victory.

26:9. The inhabitants of The world, living and dead, will learn righteousness when the Lord's judgments are in the earth.

26:19. When the earth casts out her dead none will longer need to go into death.

27:1-6. Evidences that the world has ended.

27:12, 13. The seventh trumpet marks the end of death.

28:18. Agreement with the grave to be ended; none to go there.

29:19-24. The meek shall increase their joy in the Lord, not gradually lose it, pogroms will be at an end and even sneaking provocateurs will come to know something of justice and truth.

30:26. Jehovah will bind up the hurt of his people.

32:8. In noble things shall the noble continue.

32:15-18. God's people shall abide in a sure dwelling place.

33:2. The Lord will be the salvation of some in the evil time.

33:6. In the Lord's times there will be stability and salvation.

33:16. Seek peace, seek righteousness; ye may never die.

33:22. Jehovah will says us. This may now be said by some.

33:24. The inhabitant shall not say, I am sick.

34:16, 17. Men shall dwell from generation to generation following the time when the Word of the Lord becomes understood.

35:1-10. This includes the thought of physical restoration of those now feeble, blind, deaf, and lame and their progress from the dying condition to that of everlasting joy.

40:1-5. Here are mirrored stupendous social changes and the straightening out of all earth's crooked and rough places. All flesh, the living, no less than the dead, shall see the glory of the Lord, come to know his glorious attribute of love.

41:1. The people shall renew their strength. They need not die.

41:17-20. The perfection of the earth as the everlasting home of man is here visioned, with is blessings of life for the needy.

42:1-7. When the time comes for the Lord to bring the prisoners out of death's prison house none need longer die.

42:16. This way of restitution will be a new way for the world, a way of life and not a way of death.

45:8. Salvation, life, shall spring forth from the earth under the beneficient reign of the new heavens.

45:17-19. Israel shall not be ashamed nor confounded, world without end. God made the earth to be man's permanent home.

45:22-24. All the ends of the earth shall be saved, in righteousness and strength.

49:6. When the Lord is for salvation unto the end of the earth that salvation will be for the living as well as the dead.

49:8. The earth is to be established and its desolate heritages inherited. God's covenant is to bless the people with life.

49:13. The Lord will have mercy upon the mourning people. 50:2. Who is able to prove that the Lord has no power to deliver man from going down into the tomb?

51:6. God's salvation shall be forever.

51:11. Sorrow and mourning shall be at an end.

51:21-23. The afflicted shall no more drink of God's wrath.

52:10. When all the ends of the earth see the salvation of our God it will include the living as well as the dead.

52:15. The sprinkling of many nations with the blood of the New Covenant will mean their healing, their life.

53:11. Christ would never be satisfied unless the time should come when those for whom he died that they might live should have the opportunity to live which he bought for them.

54:3. The seed of the Christ, i.e., Israel, is to possess the nations. It is not God's purpose that this shall be a dead inheritance.

55:3. Hear and your soul shall live - shall never die.

55:7-13. God will abundantly pardon the wicked who turn to him after the day of wrath is ended.

56:6-8. Here is pictured the reconciliation of all the world, living and dead - the gathering of the outcasts.

58:11. The righteous shall be like spring of water.

60:1-13. This entire passage speaks of the glory of ransomed Israel and the gathering of the forces of the redeemed race under their banner. This includes the living and the dead.

60:18. There shall be no more destruction in the land.

60:21. The people will all be righteous and not need to die.

61:1-5. A part of the church's commission is now to help the stricken world to put on beauty for ashes, to rejoice instead of mourn, to put on the garments of praise for the spirit of heaviness, by declaring that millions now living will never die.

62:10. The way is now being prepared for the people, a way by which they may go up to everlasting life without dying.

65:8. For the elect's sake God will not utterly destroy man.

65:17. There shall be a new earth, one in which man do not die.

65:20. The houses and vineyards of the people will be their permanent possession. They need not die and leave them

.66:18,19. When all nations see God's glory, there will be millions then living that will see it likewise and will not need to die. The glory of God is his mercy, his love, his pity.

JEREMIAH

3:12-18. Israel shall have knowledge and understanding and no more walk after the imagination of an evil heart. This will be true of all others, living and dead, who become Israelites.

4:1, 2. All nations shall bless themselves in becoming Israel's seed and all shall see God's glory, and not need to pass into death.

8:14. An evidence that the world has ended.

15:19-21. Fleshly Israel will stand before the Lord in the time of trouble and be delivered from all her enemies. By extension this will include millions of others now living.

16:15,18. Evidence that the world has ended.

16:19. The nations will all come to Israel to learn the truth in the new age, that they may live.

18:7, 8. Any nation that shall repent may be spared from the evil prophesied against it.

23:3, 4. Evidences that the world has ended.

24:6, 7. Israel (and others with him) shall be builded and not pulled down, planted and not plucked up.

25:11, 12. A reference to the seventy jubilees that must pass over Israel before they really enter the promised land. These 3,500 years began with the entrance into Canaan in the spring of 1575 B.C. and will end in the spring of 1925 A.D. That is to say, the last year will be a jubilee year and the last year of the 3,500 years will witness the antitype, the great jubilee of restitution.

29:14. Evidences that the world has ended.

30:3. Evidences that the world has ended.

30:18. Evidences that the world has ended.

30:23. Evidences that the world has ended.

31:6-12. Evidences that the world has ended

31:15-17. When Rachel's children return from the land of the enemy there will be millions of other children that need not die.

31:29, 30. None will die except those who sin wilfully.

31:34-37. All shall know the Lord. The nation of Israel shall never cease from being a nation.

32:39, 40. The people will have one heart and one way and God will not cease to do them good.

33:1-14. Millions now living will never die.

46:16. Evidence of the end of the world.

46:27, 28. Israel, and by extension the world, shall be in rest, at ease and no longer afraid of going into death.

49:11. Certain ones are to be preserved alive in the evil time.

50:4, 5. God's perpetual covenant with Israel, and by extension the world, looks to the time when death will end.

LAMENTATIONS

3:52-56. Evidence that the world has ended.

EZEKIEL

1:15. Evidence that the world has ended.

2:3, 9. Evidence that the world has ended.

3:15, 21. Evidence that the world has ended.

4:5, 6. Evidence that the world has ended.

7:16, 19. Evidence that the world has ended.

8:3. Evidence that the world has ended.

9:2. Evidence that the world has ended.

11:17-19. Evidence that the world has ended, also of God's purpose to recreate fleshly Israel, and by extension the world, in righteousness to the and that they need not die.

14:21. Evidence that the world has ended.

16:53-63. God's promised recovery of the Sodomites out of death and to righteousness argues that millions living need never die.

18:1-32. This entire chapter contains direct evidence that the time will come when none will need to die.

20:33-44. Evidence that the world has ended, also of God's purpose to turn his smile of favor and hence of life to fleshly Israel and, by extension, to the world.

21:15. 25-27, 31. Evidence that the world has ended.

24:16. Evidence that the world has ended.

28:26. The people are to dwell with no fear of death.

33:11-16. Direct evidence that the time will come when man shall live and not die.

33:22. Evidence that the world has ended.

34: 25-28 The people shall dwell safely and not fear death.

36:26-30, 35-38. When the people receive their new hearts and the attendant blessings none will longer need to go into death.

37:21-28. Evidence that the world has ended, because we see the regathering progress: also of God's purpose to bless the Israelites with everlasting peace from all their enemies, including the greatest of enemies, death. This, by extension, goes to all the world.

38:23. When the nations know God they will no longer die.

39:13-15, 29. When the Lord is exalted in the end of Jacob's trouble the remnant will not need to go into death.

47:9. This story about the river of life shows that when it flows the people then living need never die.

DANIEL

2:34, 35. Evidences of the end of the world.

2:44, 45. The kingdom of life, when established, will be unending. None living then need ever die.

5:25, 26. Evidence that the world has ended.

7:26, 27. The dominion of papal power has been taken away and is being consumed, and about to be destroyed. To take its place we are shortly to have an everlasting dominion under the whole heavens which will bless all the obedient with life everlasting.

8:25. The papal beast is now standing up against the Prince of princes and is immediately to be broken without hand. The world has ended; his power is forever at an end.

12:1,4, 12. Evidence that the world has ended.

HOSEA

2:13. Evidence that the world has ended.

2:14, 15. A door of hope is opened that the world may not die.
2:18-23. When the people are betrothed to the Lord in faithfulness they will no longer go into death.

3:5. When men fear the Lord and his goodness it shows such a heart relationship as will make their continuous life assured.

6:1. 2. Chronological evidence that the world has ended, and that the time for continuous life is here.

6:9. Evidence that the world has ended.

8:8-10. Evidence that the world has ended.

10:12. When the Lord rains righteousness upon the people it will reach the living of mankind first.

13:14. Death is to be destroyed out of the earth.

JOEL

1:15. Evidence that the world has ended.

2:2. Evidence that the world has ended.

2:23-32. When the Lord pours out his spirit upon all flesh none then living need ever die.

3:9, 10. Evidence that the world has ended.

AMOS

5:4. A direct statement that some need never die.

5:8. A direct statement that God will turn the shadow of death into the morning and that hence many now living need never die.

5:14, 15. A remnant is promised the gift of continued life.

8:11. 12. Evidence that the world has ended.

9:11-15. Israel (and so the world) is to plant vineyards and eat the fruit and not to be pulled up any more, not even by death.

OBADIAH

17-21. When the saviors come up on Mount Zion they will save Israel and all the world from death and every evil thing.

JONAH

3:4. An evidence that the world has ended.

3:10. Repentance is the way to life. Some may find this way.

4:11. This preservation of Nineveh from destruction fitly represents the passing over of some in the end of this age.

MICAH

1:2-4. Evidences that the world has ended.

3:6, 7. This prophetic blindness of the clergy has come to pass.

4:1-8. They shall sit under their own vines and fig trees, no longer afraid even of death, for it shall not come near them.

MICAH

7:16-20. God will pass by the transgression of the remnant of the heritage; they need not die; a direct statement.

NAHUM

1:15. When the wicked are cut off others will be spared. 2:3-6. Evidence that the world has ended.

HABAKKUK

1:12. "We shall not die."

2:1. Evidence that the world has ended.

2:14. When the earth is thus filled with the knowledge of God none will longer need to die.

3:2-6. In the day of wrath God will remember mercy.

3:12-16. When the earth is filled with the knowledge of the love of God none will longer need to die.

ZEPHANIAH

1:14-17. Evidence that the world has ended.

2:2, 3. Some will be hid in the day of the Lord's anger.

2:11. All false gods will be destroyed; the people will all serve the true God and not need to go into death.

3:8-20. This entire passage is all in sympathetic harmony with the thought that millions now living will never die.

HAGGAI

2:7. The desire of all nations is life; and it will come.

ZECHARIAH

2:10-13. The Lord will dwell in the midst of the people, bringing the blessing of life for which they long.

3:10. When every man loves his neighbor as himself none will need to die.

8:3-15. Blessings promised to the remnant of the people.

8:21-23. Evidence that the world has ended.

9:9-12. Chronological evidence that the world has ended.

9:16, 17. When the prisoners of hope are saved the salvation will also extend to those in the prison yard as well as in the tombs.

10:8-12. Israel (and so all the world) is redeemed and is to be restored and strengthened and to live with her children.

13:8, 9. The third part is to be brought through the fire.

14:8-11. When the Lord is king over all the earth none will longer need to die. There shall be no more utter destruction.

14: 16-20. When holiness is so general to the earth that men are glad to travel with signs on their harnesses "Holiness unto the Lord" the time for death will have passed.

MALACHI

1:11. When in every place heart adoration is offered unto the Lord none will longer need to die.

3:1-3. Evidence that the world has ended.

3:7, 16-18. There is coming a day when the world will turn about and see things from the divine viewpoint, and cease dying.

4:1-6. Evidence that the world has ended and that millions now living will "grow up as calves of the stall".

MATTHEW

5:1. The meek shall inherit the earth; they shall not die.

7:27. Evidence that the world has ended.

8:11. The living shall participate in the kingdom.

8:26. Representing the great calm following the time of trouble.

11:28. The weary, heave laden world will find rest in the new king. They will be no longer burdened by the fear of death.

12:20. The work of the judgment day, now begun, is for the very purpose of preventing the utter extinguishment of life.

13:48. Evidence that the world has ended.

17:11. Evidence that the world has ended.

18:11. The Son of man came to save the dying world, not to destroy. When he reigns death is no more.

19:16. The privilege of living on into the new era will be possible for those who take advantage of the means then open.

19:30. Many who are last upon the earth prior to the kingdom will be first to be blessed.

20:8. 16. Evidence that the world has ended.

20:28. A ransom for all means an opportunity for all and this will be granted to both the living and the dead in his due time.

22:11,13. Evidence that the world has ended.

22:32. God is a god of the living and when his time comes to give life to the dead he will surely not overbook those then living.

24:1-51. Entire chapter is evidence that the world has ended.

25:5. Evidence that the world has ended.

25:19. Evidence that the world has ended.

25:31, 32, 46. The living, as well as the dead, will share in this classification and in the promised reward of eternal life.

26:28. When the blood is applied on behalf of the many, millions now living need never die.

MARK

3:26. Evidence that the world has ended.

9:12. Evidence that the world has ended.

10:31. Many who are last upon earth prior to the kingdom will be first to be blessed.

13:10. Evidence that the world has ended.

13:19. Evidence that the world has ended.

13:20. The days will be shortened and some flesh will be saved.

LUKE

2:10, 14. 22. The glad tidings of life will be to all people, living and dead, when the due time has come.

3:7-11. These warnings to fleshly Israel are appropriate to be given now to nominal spiritual Israel to the end of their age.

11:2. The doing of God's will on earth as it is done in heaven implies that death will some time be no more.

12:32. Those who are to be saved with the heavenly salvation will be but a little flock, but they shall have myriads of subjects.

13:28-30. The living shall participate in the kingdom.

15:11-32. The parable of the prodigal son shows the world's recovery from sin and death, beginning with those now living.

17:26-30. Evidence that the world has ended; also, Noah and Lot did not die in their times of trouble.

18:8. Evidence that the world has ended.

19:10. The Lord comes at his second advent to give life to those he redeemed at his first advent.

19:27. Those who are willing the king shall reign over them will not be slain. 21:24, 25, 29-33. Evidence that the world has ended.

JOHN

1:4-9. Every man that ever lived is to be enlightened and, appropriately,. this enlightenment will begin with the living

3:15, 16 It is not God's will that any should perish.

4:36. Evidence that the world has ended.

5:25-29. When all that are in their graves hear his voice and come forth none will longer need to die.

6:5, 47-51, 58. This great multitude that was fed with literal bread represents the world, living and dead, that will be given life

8:51, 52. Some will never taste of death.

10:10. Christ has come that they may have life, not death.

11:25, 26. At the proper time, those believing shall never die.

12:32. All men, living and dead, are to be drawn to the Lord.

17:2. Christ's power over all flesh will result in eternal life to living as well as dead.

21:4, 5. 6. In the morning of the Millennial day there will be a great ingathering, but both of the living and the dead.

ACTS

1:6. When the kingdom is restored to Israel death will end.
2:16-21. Evidence that the world has ended and that millions who call upon the name of the Lord shall be saved from death.

3:19-21. Times of refreshing accompany the times of restitution.

7:21, 30. 36. Chronological evidence that the world has ended.

7:37. A reference to the great Deliverer of living and dead.

10:42, 43. During the judgment day, now here, the Lord will judge (uplift and bless) both the living and the dead.

13:38, 39. The forgiveness and justification here referred do will be operative toward both the living and the dead.

13:47. The Lord will be the salvation of all, living and dead.

15:13-18. After the people for the Lord's name have been selected and his ruined kingdom has been re-established in the earth, the ultimate purpose, the blessing of the residue of man, living and dead, with the gift of life, will be manifested.

17:30, 31. A blessed assurance to the living and the dead.

24:15. This restanding of the unjust for which the apostle hoped will be operative toward the living as well as the dead.

ROMANS

2:10. These blessings coming to the Jews and afterwards to the Gentiles will be for the living as well as the dead.

3:26. The Lord Jesus will be justifier of living as well as dead.

5:17-19. When the "many" are made righteous it will include the living as well as the dead.

6:23. This gift of God will be extended to the living as well as the dead when the New Covenant goes into operation.

8:5. The law could not give life to the weak Jews but Jesus can do so, and, by extension, to all, living and dead.

8:19-23. When the creation ceases to groan, as a result of the manifestation of the Sons of God, Jesus and his body-members, the blessings then due will be for both living and dead.

10:13-21. When the message of the gospel does go into all the world and when Israel does know the truth, as herein prophesied, all who shall call upon the name of the Lord shall be saved.

11:26-32. When all Israel is saved the salvation will extend to others, living and dead, as they come under the New Covenant.

16:20. When Satan is bruised under the feet of the Christ, salvation will follow to all the living and the dead.

1. CORINTHIANS

6:2. When the saints judge the world (for their uplifting) this judging work will begin with the living and, in a sense, now is.

15:20-23. When the due time for all to be made alive is here it will not be longer necessary for any to go into death.

2. CORINTHIANS

5:15. Christ died for all and the blessings of his ransom price will be extended to all, living and dead.

5: 18-20. When, as a result of the world's trespasses being imputed to our Lord, he offers them the gift of life under the New Covenant. that gift will be for the living as well as the dead.

GALATIANS

3:8. When all the nations are blessed the living will participate.

3:29. The promise is that all the nations shall be blessed.

EPHESIANS

1:10-14. When Christ gathers together all the earthly things in himself it will include the living as well as the dead. All mankind are his purchased possession.

PHILIPPIANS

2:9-11. When every knee bows end every tongue confesses that Jesus Christ is Lord of his heart death will be no more.

3:21. When God subdues all men, bringing them unto himself, his work will include the living, as well as the dead.

COLOSSIANS

1:20. It is God's purpose to reconcile to himself all men.

1. THESSALONIANS

4:16. This is a shout of encouragement for both living and dead.
5:3,4. Evidence that the world has ended.

2. THESSALONIANS

1:9, 10. The Lord will be admired by the whole world, living and dead, in his Millennial day, now at hand.
2:3-9. Evidences that the world has ended.

1. TIMOTHY

2:3-6. When Christ Jesus' due time has come that his ransom be testified to all men, it will reach the living first.
4:1-3. Evidence that the world has ended.
4:9-11. God is the savior of all, living and dead.

2. TIMOTHY

2:20. When the earthen vessels in God's great house of the universe are being put in order the work will begin with those living.
3: 1-5, 9. Evidence that the world has ended.
4:1-4. Evidence that the world has ended

TITUS

2:11-14. When God's grace that brings salvation to all men appears to the world it will come first to the living.

HEBREWS

2:7-9. The original plan is to be carried out. The first feature or step toward the carrying out of the plan is the death of Jesus as man's ransom price. The return of the dominion will follow.
6:2. During the "age-lasting judgment" day referred to in this text the first to be blessed will be the living.
7:19-27. The old Law Covenant brought perfect life to none, but the new Law Covenant will accomplish what the first could not.

8:6, 10. Another reference to the better covenant. See above.

9:7. The typical offering on behalf of all the people of Israel represented Christ's offering for all the people, living and dead.

9:26-28. The first to "look for him" will be the living, followed, every man in his own order, by all the dead.

10:16. The rewriting of the law of love in the hearts of men will begin with the living first.

11:39, 40. An earthly salvation is provided for some, and obviously will be first presented to those living when it has arrived.

12:22-27. Evidence that the world has ended.

JAMES

5:1-5. Evidence that the world has ended.

1. PETER

2:12. The day of visitation of the world will be the Millennial day and the first ones thus "visited will be the living

2. PETER

3:1-13. Evidence that the world has ended.

1. JOHN

2:2. Inasmuch as Jesus' death was the propitiation or satisfaction for the sins of the whole world it follows that the whole world, living and dead, have a direct interest in it and will share the gift of life thereby purchased. These blessings will be available to both the living and the dead, and to the living first.

2:17, 18. Evidence that the world has ended.

JUDE

6, 17, 18. Evidence that the world has ended.

REVELATION

1:18. Our Lord has the key of death for a purpose, and that purpose is to unlock the prison-house, both for those already in the prison itself and those in the courtyard of the prison, those in the grave and those on the way thither.

4:10. These elders may now be discerned in this very act.

5:10. God's kingdom is to be re-established in the earth and its subjects will be the living and the dead - the living first.

6:12-17. Evidence that the world has ended.

8:1. Evidence that the world has ended.

10:3, 7. Evidence that the world has ended.

11:17, 18. Evidence that the world has ended.

14:6, 10, 20. Evidence that the world has ended.

15:3. Evidence that the world has ended.

15:4. This promise to all nations will be to the living first.

15:6. Evidence that the world has ended.

16:13-21. Evidence that the world has ended.

17:12-18. Evidence that the world has ended.

18:1-24. Evidence the world has ended.

20:3. Evidence that the world has ended.

20:12. This trial of the world will be for the benefit of those dead in trespasses and sins as well as those actually dead.

20:13. The sea here apparently is a symbolic sea, and seemingly offers direct evidence that the first to be reached by the kingdom blessings will be those who have been through the time of trouble.

21:1-7. Evidence that the world has ended and that million now living will never die.

21:24. This bringing of the nations into light and life will be for the living nations first.

22:2, 3. The healing of the nations will be for the living nations first. When the curse is removed none will longer need to die.

22:17. When the spirit and the bride say, Come, they will say it first to those then living and subsequently to all-mankind. There is every reason to believe that, when the due time has come for the bride to extend this massage to mankind, none of those who hear and heed the message need longer go into death.

www.ingramcontent.com/pod-product-compliance
Lightning Source LLC
LaVergne TN
LVHW050938080826
845145LV00004B/1315

* 9 7 8 1 7 8 9 8 7 2 8 6 6 *